Harry Stack Sullivan and Anton T. Boisen: Comrades and Revolutionaries in Psychotherapy

Harry Stack Sullivan and Anton T. Boisen

Comrades and Revolutionaries in Psychotherapy

Raymond J. Lawrence

IPBOOKS.net
International Psychoanalytic Books

International Psychoanalytic Books (IPBooks)
New York • http://www.IPBooks.net

Harry Stack Sullivan and Anton T. Boisen:
Comrades and Revolutionaries in Psychotherapy

Published by IPBooks, Queens, NY
Online at: www.IPBooks.net

Cover photo of Harry Stack Sullivan reprinted with permission of the Washington School of Psychiatry
Cover photo Anton Boisen reprinted with permission of the Kansas State Historical Society

ISBN: 978-1-956864-11-3

For Jennifer Harper

who like Freud, Sullivan and Boisen

has done so much to empower religious leaders

to assume their historic role as healers of the human spirit.

CONTENTS

———

AUTHOR'S ACKNOWLEDGEMENTS

I am astonished that I personally invested some half a century of professional work in training pastors and other religious workers in clinical pastoral skills but only near the end of my career discovered the critical details of the actual story of the founder of the clinical pastoral training movement, Anton T. Boisen, and in particular, his long and significant relationship with Harry Stack Sullivan, whom I will call "The American Freud". I did not realize for most of my professional life that Boisen's life had been revised for public relations purposes. I of course must be held accountable for lacking an appropriate level of curiosity through most of my working years in permitting myself to remain in the dark. But for what it's worth, I was hardly alone. Virtually all of my colleagues worked in similar unawareness. It is now clear that this century-long movement inaugurated by Boisen, which radically altered religious work, gradually but successfully erased, or radically revised the memory of Boisen's authentic contribution to religion and mental health. Subsequent history has treated Boisen similarly to history's treatment of Sullivan. His name was preserved, but the substance of his contribution to history, monumental though it was, is forgotten. Both Boisen's and Sullivan's name among their fellow professionals became what it is now—an empty shell. My purpose in this monograph was to recover and restore our corporate memory of the authentic Anton Theophilus Boisen, my fellow professional, and also to add my voice to the very small coterie of psychiatrists who properly credit Sullivan with transforming psychiatry.

So many have assisted me in large and small ways to complete this monograph. The current executive leadership and staff of the College of Pastoral Supervision and Psychotherapy have been stalwart, namely Bryan Jones, Patty Berron, Cynthia Olson, David Plummer, Juan T. Loya, Charles Kirby, Asnel Valcin, Parthenia Cesar and Krista Argiropolis. Others who have aided me in large and small ways were Perry N. Miller, Solon Smith, David Roth, Ruth Kuo and Yasmine Abou-el-Kheir. F. Barton Evans and Robert Charles Powell, reliable authorities on Sullivan and Boisen respectively, have encouraged me along in many ways, as well as set me straight from time to time. Three copy editors in succession have been extremely helpful, encouraging, and essential in making this monograph both more readable and more accurate: Howard Pendley, Carol Skolnic, and last but not least, Cynthia Olson. To each of them I am indebted and very grateful.

INTRODUCTION

This monograph unearths a century-long secret, the quarter-century relationship between Harry Stack Sullivan and Anton T. Boisen that began in 1924 and ended with Sullivan's death in 1949. We know only a little about the contours of the relationship. But we do know that they were good friends and that they held each other in mutual esteem. There is some suggestion that Sullivan was the dominant one of the pair, but that is not well documented. There is very little left written that describes with precision what they each meant to the other. Most of the surviving letters reveal little more than when they planned to meet. But Boisen did have the unambiguous public endorsement of Sullivan himself, a monumental authorization for any cleric. That the pastoral world and the world of psychiatry lost memory of this relationship is unsurprising. Sullivan, for all his many radical and creative innovations, who left his distinct mark on virtually all subsequent psychiatry, was not much appreciated by the members of his own profession. The minute he died, psychiatry deliberately lost memory of him as the game-changer that he was in his profession. One might even say that psychiatry purposefully suppressed any memory of him. And to this day, almost three-quarters of a century later, Sullivan remains essentially unread and unknown. Anton Boisen suffered a different but substantially similar fate. Unlike Sullivan, his name continues to be venerated in the clinical pastoral

1

world, the world of clinical chaplains and pastoral psychotherapists, but the substance of his revolution has been entirely gutted through the years. Boisen's books went out of print decades ago. Few read him today. He was rarely cited in his discipline except as a kind of mantra. But the fact is that both Boisen and Sullivan spawned a radical revolution in their respective professions—psychiatry and pastoral work—and yet the work of these two revolutionaries remains essentially unknown in the fields they served. Thus, both Sullivan and Boisen were posthumous victims of almost total amnesia in their own disciplines, which is a remarkable turn of events. Yet each of these unknown men radically altered his chosen profession in his own lifetime.

The precise years that both these men prospered was the quarter-century between 1923 and 1948. Boisen himself lived on sixteen years subsequent to Sullivan's death. However, the aging process, illness and possibly the absence of Sullivan appeared to stunt his effectiveness. Boisen did not age well.

Also of note is the fact that both men suffered some degree of schizophrenia. Boisen's several episodes were documented both institutionally and in his own writing. Sullivan's were not disclosed, but were revealed posthumously by some who knew him well and loved him.

❖ ❖ ❖

I began my career in the clinical pastoral movement in the 1960s. As many others did at that time, I studied the permeable boundary between religion and psychiatry, following the tradition of Boisen, which was still alive in the 1960s. My mentors in the Boisen movement considered themselves "pastoral psychotherapists." Consequently, I read a good deal in the field of psychiatry in its various iterations, beginning with Sigmund Freud, but including a wide range of his later followers in the discipline. The name Harry Stack Sullivan rarely—almost never—came up on my screen, or was referenced by a particular psychiatric authority or pastoral clinician, or in any literature that I might be reading. And when his name did appear, it was in the context of his being yet another psychiatrist of relatively minor importance, not in such a way as to stir my interest. Furthermore, Sullivan was never in my experience portrayed as even slightly important to Boisen and his pastoral psychotherapy movement. And Sullivan was never cited as a psychiatrist of significance in the company of Sigmund Freud, Sandor Ferenczi, Earnest Jones, Anna Freud, Eric Fromm, Robert S. Wallerstein, Stephen Mitchell, Wilfred Bion, Donald W. Winnicott, or any other such luminaries whom I encountered. Thus I never read a word of Sullivan in my half century of study and of training clergy in the art and skill of pastoral psychotherapy. And I read precious little even of Boisen himself. I am confident that my course of reading and training was also typical of my peers at mid-century. In retrospect I now see how astonishing this is.

The truth is that the name of Harry Stack Sullivan belongs right next to the name of Sigmund Freud. They each radically altered the world they lived in.

❖ ❖ ❖

I believe that what first called my attention to Sullivan was the circumstantial discovery of an article written by Boisen and published in *Psychiatry,* a journal founded by and edited by Sullivan himself. I followed the string, and it led me to the library of the Chicago Theological Seminary, which houses the documents left by Boisen. The librarian, Yasmine Abou el Kheir, very graciously made Boisen's letters and other documents available to me and assisted me in other ways as well. What I found was an enormous surprise—namely, that Boisen and Sullivan were personal friends and professional colleagues and remained in close contact, by mail, by phone, and face-to-face meetings, from 1924 until Sullivan's death in January, 1949. This

3

monograph lays out the parameters of that relationship as far as I am able to reconstruct them. Unfortunately, a great deal is missing, namely, the content of their discussions in their many meetings. That they were personally close is irrefutable. What their differences were seems likewise irrefutable to an outsider but how they negotiated their differences is not clear, and likely lost to history. But in spite of their differences, their positive and mutually affirming relationship stayed on course for a quarter-century until Sullivan's death.

What I attempt to do in this monograph is to elaborate their connections, summarize the nature of their work respectively, and delineate areas of differences.

❖ ❖ ❖

"I offer (my own case record) as a case of valid religious experience which was at the same time madness of the most profound and unmistakable variety." Boisen[1]

"To be plunged as a patient into a hospital for the insane may be a tragedy or it may be an opportunity. For me it has been an opportunity." Boisen[2]

"Gods keep you."—Sullivan's typical parting words.[3]

"In the family myth the Sullivans were considered descendants of the West Wind, riding east to meet the dawn."[4]

"Most of us have but the peace and quiet of fresh thistledown on a windy day." Sullivan[5]

CHAPTER 1

The Beginning

⌒∞⌒

Religious and psychotherapeutic authorities in the twentieth century and later have had a persistent problem with both Harry Stack Sullivan and Anton Boisen. Both men were game changers in their respective professions, and radical ones at that. The two men significantly altered the terms of the debate on the question of what constitutes healing of the human mind and soul. The same kinds of authorities had a similar problem somewhat earlier with another game changer: Sigmund Freud. But Freud was never forgotten; however, many attempted to forget him. Furthermore, and remarkably, much of the resistance to all three men was driven by discomfort over issues of sexuality. The source of that discomfort was the profound negativity toward sexual pleasure that had permeated Western culture for about 17 centuries, an odd posture that seems to have been unique among the cultures of the world. Its most articulate author was St. Augustine of Hippo, although he did not invent this stance. Its roots were linked to elements of earlier Greek and Roman culture, but Augustine became the preeminent voice for shaming the marital beds of all Westerners ever since. No religion, nor any psychology, has been able to successfully shake off this curse; Martin Luther in the sixteenth century was temporarily successful, when with open delight, he married Katie the nun, not so much because of his own libido as to support others with their own (and also out of his desire to stick his finger in the eye of the

Pope). He thus dramatically overturned sexual negativism and reasserted a quite Jewish affirmation of sexual pleasure, supported by a more faithful translation and reading of the biblical texts. But Luther's victory was short-lived. His protégés—the Lutherans and other Protestants—gradually erased it in favor of a conventional, middle class sexual valorization. Indeed, and ironically, the subsequent Protestant movement soon reverted to a position on sexuality *almost* as negative as that of St. Augustine himself. [6]

The Jewish people, along with their sexually affirming sacred texts, have consistently and remarkably remained relatively uncontaminated by this Christian curse of sex guilt, which is likely indeed to be the hidden or unconscious source of persistent and virulent antisemitism. The Mishnah—the Jewish text defining proper behavior, compiled during an extended period of time before and after the onset of Christendom—was unabashedly and unambiguously affirming of sexual pleasure outside the Imperial Roman boundaries of monogamy. Its sequel, the Talmud, was created in later centuries, but continued the spirit of the sex-affirming Mishna. Certainly the secular Jew, Sigmund Freud, boldly penetrated the Christian anti-sexual fortress, but he paid a price for that, and is still paying, posthumously.

Neither of the two preeminent authorities on psychotherapy in the twentieth century—Freud, a non-observant Jew, nor Harry Stack Sullivan, a fallen-away Catholic—had any investment in religion as such; they were both negative toward religion in general, giving their attention to matters of psychological health. Religion was at best peripheral to them, and typically antithetical to their mission. They approached sexual issues strictly from a scientific, psychological, therapeutic, and humanistic perspective. Opinion makers in the quasi-Christian culture took some notice, but not much. (Sullivan was laudatory about Quakerism, seeing it as probably the highest form of religion. But he also is reported to have appreciated the austerity, unemotionality, and impersonal beauty of the Catholic mass as an art form. That seems to have been the extent of his appreciation of formal religion.) [7]

Early in the twentieth century, on the heels of Sigmund Freud, there were two principal figures in the United States who took up Freud's mantle and, in a radical fashion, reframed his therapeutic, and made it accessible to the common people. The first was Harry Stack Sullivan, who laicized psychotherapy and trained relatively uneducated persons to perform lay psychotherapy. The second was Anton T. Boisen, a Protestant minister who, with Sullivan's help, trained run-of-the-mill pastors to become pastoral psychotherapists. Subsequently leaders in many other manifestations of religion joined in.

Thus Boisen, a Protestant pastor and a most unlikely follower of either Freud or Sullivan, became a serious and long-time adept of both. Sexually repressed personally, to an extraordinary extent he should have been expected to denounce both men. However, Boisen, a sometime psychotic himself, had concerns about his own sanity. His vision of assisting others who experienced psychological problems trumped ideology. He laid aside the disdain for religion found in both Freud and Sullivan, and even more astonishing, he laid aside their sexual libertinism in order to sit at their feet, so to speak. It is not a little ironic that the central religious innovator of the twentieth-century American religious community, with its phobic posture toward sexual pleasure, was empowered by no less than teachings of Freud and Sullivan.

While neither Sullivan nor Boisen had ever met Freud in person, each was profoundly inspired by him, and studied his writings. On that platform, they bonded, and became the most unlikely of friends and professional colleagues for over a quarter century. The calendar was perhaps against Sullivan and Boisen connecting with Freud personally: by 1930, when they were flowering professionally, Freud was in serious physical decline with cancer of the jaw and died in 1939. But another, more likely reason for their never meeting with Freud was perhaps the fear of being dominated by the giant in the context of any interpersonal engagement.

9

Strangely enough, the two men were almost exact contemporaries vocationally, beginning and ending their professionally productive years simultaneously. They met in 1924, the year Boisen began work as Chaplain at Worcester State Psychiatric Hospital, in Massachusetts, and Sullivan was directing a psychiatric ward at Sheppard Pratt, near Baltimore. Sullivan was 32; Boisen was 49. Each would find his sea legs in short order, and they each effected radical changes in their respective professions. Sullivan died in 1949 at age 56. Boisen lived on another 16 years, to age 89, but he was not very productive beyond his 70s and subsequent to Sullivan's death in 1949.

At the turn of the twentieth century, Freud achieved public attention for his new healing approach, psychotherapy and psychoanalysis. Intrinsic to his therapeutic process was a laser focus on the sexual life of men and women. In response, Christian authorities took note and alarm bells sounded in the sex-phobic Christian culture. But paradoxically, a countervailing wind was blowing, signaling an affirmation of Freud's message. His thesis struck a chord with Anton Boisen, who knew at some level that his own episodic psychoses were related to sexuality. And through Boisen, supported by Sullivan, Freudian theory seeped *sotto voce* into the American religious community by way of his newly created *clinical pastoral training* movement. The result of Boisen's mission was the radical transformation of pastoral work in twentieth-century America. Pastors became *de facto* psychotherapists, though later they mostly pulled their punches and devalued themselves by accepting the label "Pastoral Counselor," an identifier less threatening to the medical establishment, which had determined—quite arrogantly, and in defiance of Sullivan—that any healing of either mind or body would be directed exclusively by the medical profession. It was at root a war over turf and income. By the last quarter of the twentieth century, it was clear that Sullivan's and Boisen's fingers-in-the-dyke defense against medical hegemony had lost the battle. For the rest of the century, the medicalization of all psychotherapy resulted in amnesia about even the existence of Sullivan and

Boisen, and especially their accomplishments. By the end of the twentieth century, their respective personhoods had faded into an inchoate blur. [8]

The parameters and details of the 25-year-long friendship between Sullivan and Boisen are mostly lost to history. Neither man seems to have kept much in the way of private notes describing their relationship. However, with the few existing letters and statements, there is enough surviving historical data at least to document the strong bond between them.

While significantly indebted to Freud, Boisen continued to be troubled by Freud's sexual libertinism, although never quite enough to separate himself from Freudian theory and practice. In the final analysis, Boisen owned his debt to Freud, as he expressed a year before his death to Henri Nouwen during a bedside visit. He shared with Nouwen the salvific nature of Freud's writing for him personally, from which he was inspired to create the *clinical pastoral training* movement. [9]

Unlike his impersonal relationship with Freud, Boisen was *personally* close to Sullivan. Sullivan was every bit as much of a sexual free thinker as Freud, if not more so, while Boisen was as sexually constrained as Augustine and equally pathological in his assessment of sexual pleasure of any sort. This issue never seemed to have disturbed the quarter-century relationship between the two men—at least, there is no indication of it—during which time Boisen was highly resistant personally to Freud's seeming sexual libertinism, even as he remained deeply indebted to his basic theory.

Meanwhile, many others in Boisen's movement were increasingly sympathetic to Freud's posture on sex, at some risk to their professional status. One of Boisen's preeminent protégés, the openminded Wayne Oates, wrote his Ph.D. thesis on Freud. He intended to publish it, demurring only when his colleagues warned him that any public identification with Freud would forever ruin him and his reputation in the wider Baptist community. However, he continued to teach Freud's doctrines *sub rosa*, and was largely successful in that; many of his best trainees, such as Myron Madden and

Don Cabaniss, also Southern Baptist ministers, became noted authorities on Freud. Strange as it may seem, each actually taught Freudian psychoanalysis to medical residents at Tulane University in New Orleans and at Central State Hospital in Milledgeville, Georgia, respectively, in the 1960s. By then, they had enough allies to be able to marshal a defense.

For the most part, however, Freudian theory was driven underground in the wider American religious community. Both psychotherapy and psychoanalysis remained captive of scientific medicine, a turn of events that would have dismayed Freud. The disciplines themselves were much identified with Freud in the public mind, and rightfully so: It was, after all, Freud who originated psychoanalytic thinking. David Roberts, a Union Seminary professor and member of the distinguished "New York Psychology Group" in the 1940s, confessed to Allison Stokes, a key historian of the Boisen movement, that he had made a mistake in publishing his first book, *Psychotherapy and a Christian View of Man*, because he was thereafter pegged as "a psychotherapy man." From the mainstream Christian point of view, that was far from a compliment. [10] Roberts thereby absorbed the negative public innuendo that had been projected onto Freud. Wayne Oates told Stokes that he himself had studied Wilhelm Reich, Harry Stack Sullivan, Carl Rogers, and the like, but that he had pulled his punch on emphasizing Freud in his teaching of seminarians because "more history is on the way." [11] What he really meant was that the public price for being known as a Freudian in his lifetime, or even a fellow traveler, would be so costly that he likely would not be able to work with churches at all. And he was surely correct.

It is time now for the "more history" to which Oates alluded that has been on the way for almost a century: the long-awaited decision of religious leaders to declare themselves authentic psychotherapists in the Freudian–Sullivanian–Boisenian tradition, and full-throatedly to take on that task. The hand-on-the-head prayers to Jesus, the Virgin Mary, or the saints hocus-pocus has no credible history of therapeutic bona fides. But it seems likely that most religious leaders will continue on in that vein as pretend-healers, propagandists, and community organizers, which are currently the typical clerical long suits. However, those religious leaders who want to be genuine healers will go back to Freud, Boisen, Sullivan, and the increasingly numerous band of their followers. Donald Capps pointed the way forward in his monograph, *Jesus the Village Psychiatrist.* [12] Jesus himself, according to Capps, was a precursor to Sigmund Freud. Jesus' healings, wrote Capps, were of the same order as Freud's healing of Elizabeth von R., for example, who lost her ability to walk. She sought out Freud for treatment, and in due course was later seen dancing a waltz in Vienna. The paralyzed woman now dancing a stunning meme echoing the Jesus story. And note that neither Freud nor Jesus were Christians, but Jews.

Anton Boisen created a bold path forward, even if he did so on tenterhooks. Against all odds, he followed Freud for the most part and he paired himself significantly and personally with Harry Stack Sullivan. Thus Boisen identified with both the founder of psychotherapy and with the preeminent American psychotherapist and psychoanalyst of the twentieth century. Boisen did indeed exhibit ambivalence; he was never quite prepared to purchase Freud's or Sullivan's unambiguously positive valorization of sexual pleasure both within and without the marital contract. But somehow, he put his own neurotic fear of sex on the back burner and became an avowed Freudian as well as a Sullivanian. The details of those relationships are elaborated on, insofar as they are accessible to us, in this monograph.

Boisen's Literary Corpus:

Anton T. Boisen listed his published works at the end of *Out of The Depths,* itself published in 1960, his last book. He had published four other books in his lifetime: *The Exploration of the Inner World* (1936), *Religion in Crisis and Custom* (1945/1955), *Problems in Religion and Life* (1946), and *Hymns of Hope and Courage* (1950). He also published a number of journal articles: in the journal *Psychiatry* (nine articles), the *American Journal of Sociology* (three articles), the *American Journal of Psychiatry* (two articles), and one each in the *American Review, Social Action, Bulletin of the Massachusetts Department of Mental Diseases;* as well as a great number of articles in a variety of religious and theological journals.

Sullivan's Literary Corpus

Harry Stack Sullivan wrote two books. The first, *Personal Psychopathology,* was written between 1929 and 1933, but was "Privately Circulated" and did not make a public appearance in his lifetime. It was finally published posthumously, nearly two decades later, in 1965, with an "Introduction" by Helen Swick Perry. *Conceptions of Modern Psychiatry* was Sullivan's only book published in his lifetime, and it had a peculiar history. Its first iteration was as a publication of the five lectures from the First William Alanson White Memorial Lectures in 1939. That collection was edited and published in the journal *Psychiatry* in 1940, of which Sullivan himself was editor. The text continued to be distributed in pamphlet form for students, expanded, and in 1945, with a 55-page addendum by Patrick Mullahy. In 1947, a reprinting of the lectures, finally in book form, and was authorized "for the use of students." It sold 20,000 copies, a remarkable number for a psychotherapy book, let alone a privately published one. It was reviewed in the *New York Times Book Review* in 1947, and used regularly as a text in social science departments. Sullivan, who died in 1949, did not see any book of his displayed in any bookstore in his lifetime. *Conceptions* was not

14

published commercially until 1953 and was reprinted by W. W. Norton & Company, Inc.

Sullivan seems to have had significant resistance to publishing anything for public consumption, except for whatever he sent to journals of psychiatry, sociology, and anthropology, or published in his own journal, *Psychiatry,* to be read by specialists. We can only surmise why that was so. One thought is that his writing was largely incomprehensible and that he was likely aware that the common reader would not be able to follow him. Another thought is that he was very much on the cutting edge, challenging basic assumptions in psychiatry, and thus subject to serious criticism, even public ridicule. And in addition, his writings on human sexuality were countercultural enough to have gotten him lynched—literally. Therefore, he may have preferred to keep his thoughts mostly under the tent, available only to colleagues and select academic readers. Sullivan, the epitome of the creatively idiosyncratic, perhaps did not want to see his idiosyncrasies circulated in the newspapers. Another factor is that he and his ideas were in constant flux: a continuing work in progress. Perhaps he wondered if what he published today would linger around and blow back on him tomorrow, after he had had a change of mind. Of course, these are all speculative thoughts about why he published only one book at the very end of his life and have little or no substantive confirmation.

But Sullivan did write prolifically, literally thousands of pages, producing for the cognoscenti an enormous trove of papers and journal articles. He also left behind a large corpus of recorded lectures and seminars. As editor of *Psychiatry* for a decade, he also produced a very large number of editorials, as well as other pieces, many of which were published in other journals. His editorials for *Psychiatry* were typically not identified as having been written by him, which might have been another way to somewhat dissociate his name from his radical ideas. However, who but the editor of a journal writes

15

unsigned editorials? Those editorials, along with papers he wrote for other journals, and speeches he gave in various contexts, provided material for six posthumous volumes of his writings. The content and organization of these six collections was chosen by a team nominally headed by the psychiatrist David Rioch and colleagues, joined by Sullivan's former secretary, Helen Swick Perry, and are listed below in order of publication:

- *The Interpersonal Theory of Psychiatry* (1953; abbreviated hereafter as ITP) was the first posthumous book of Sullivan's writing to be published. It consists mostly of a selection of his late lectures given in the time period 1944–47. Since Sullivan changed his mind on many issues through the years, these papers could be considered the closest thing to his final opinion.
- *The Psychiatric Interview* (1954; hereafter TPI) is a collection of two series of lectures Sullivan presented in 1944 and 1945 to the William Alanson White Psychiatric Foundation and presented also at the Washington School of Psychiatry, which was the training institution of the Foundation. These lectures were recorded, presumably electronically, and the book was copied from the recordings.
- *Clinical Studies in Psychiatry* (1956; hereafter CSP) is a collection of lectures Sullivan gave at Chestnut Lodge in the middle 1940s. He gave 246 lectures over a six-year period, consisting of more than 1,000,000 words. Only 130,000 words—about 13 percent—are included in this book.
- *Schizophrenia as a Human Process* (1962; hereafter SHP) is a collection of all the major articles Sullivan wrote from the beginning of his career in 1924 until 1930.
- *The Fusion of Psychiatry and Social Science* (1964; hereafter Fusion)— which, according to Helen Swick Perry, should be considered a companion to the prior book—contains journal articles from 1937

onward. It also reflects Sullivan's close, decade-long relationship with anthropologist Edward Sapir at Yale, until Sapir's untimely death in 1939 at age 55.

Thus, these five volumes—leaving aside the two books actually written by Sullivan, *Conceptions of Modern Psychiatry* (hereafter CMP) and *Personal Psychopathology* (1965; hereafter PP)—are not technically books *by* Sullivan, but rather collections of his papers and journal articles, arranged into book form over a 15-year period by the editorial team. Much of what Sullivan wrote or recorded is not contained in any of the seven volumes. There is very likely no living person—or deceased—who has read all of Sullivan's works and heard all his recordings.

The Committee on Publication of Sullivan's writings declined to make alterations in Sullivan's difficult style. Helen Swick Perry and others included a very useful "Introduction" for most of the collections. The Publication Committee was a strong group consisting of David McKenzie Rioch (without whom Sullivan's writings would likely have languished and disappeared), Mabel Blake Cohen, Janet MacKenzie Rioch, Clara Thompson, Dexter Bullard, and later Otto Will and Donald Burnham, all psychiatrists who were personally close to Sullivan.

Sullivan also left behind an unknown amount of court reporter type notes as well as electronic recordings of his lectures at Chestnut Lodge, a distinguished treatment center during that era in Rockville, Maryland. Some of the recordings have been used to produce discussions of Sullivan's work, such as Robert G. Kvarnes' *A Harry Stack Sullivan Case Seminar: Treatment of a Young Schizophrenic.*

Sullivan and Freud

Much ink has been spilt in attempts to separate Sullivan from Freud, or even to recast them as adversaries. It is a vain undertaking. It is similar to the attempts to set up Paul and Jesus as adversaries, or Luther and Calvin, or Socrates and Plato, or Plato and Aristotle. Each member of the pair was quite different from the other, and yet very much alike, as in a dialectic. Freud and Sullivan were also very much alike. But Sullivan was no carbon copy of Freud. Even though they never met, the relationship between their ideas and theories was strong and dialectical. And they had much more in common than what separated them. At critical points, Sullivan clarified that he followed Freud and built on his theories. What else can a faithful successor to a creative person do but to build on what has already been accomplished? [13] Sullivan declared psychiatry an art, as did Freud late in life, namely "the art of observing and perhaps influencing the course of mental disorders." [14]

Sullivan also subscribed to "the postulate of the unconscious, the great contribution of Professor Freud." [15] On the other hand, Sullivan did mock the Freudians who refer to the unconscious as if they had possession of it in their pockets.

The principal way that Sullivan expanded on Freud was in his emphasis on the essential social existence of persons. Living, he asserted, cannot be separated from relationships and community without a deterioration in personality. Dorothy Blitsten, who wrote one of the very first monographs on Sullivan after his death, boldly went so far as to label Sullivan as "a social scientist whose specialty was psychiatry." [16] Sullivan even described himself among friends in such terms, as a sociologist with an interest in psychiatry. This is acted out in Sullivan's close association and friendship with Sociologist Edward Sapir at Yale and with Harold Lasswell, the father of political psychology. Sullivan, Sapir, and Lasswell planned to develop the research branch of the William Alanson White Institute, along with development of the Washington School of Psychiatry and the journal *Psychiatry*. The economic problems of the times and Sapir's inopportune death in 1939 ended the collaboration.

In Sullivan's close association with Anton Boisen, he dramatized his commitment to lay psychotherapy, in that case in the pastoral arena, echoing Freud's assertion late in life that he never really considered himself a doctor but rather "a secular pastoral worker." [17] The other major way that Sullivan expanded on Freud was his mission to work with schizophrenics, probably because Sullivan was almost certainly a sometime schizophrenic himself. Freud in 1914 considered such a diagnosis as signaling untreatability from a psychoanalytic perspective. The ability to form a transference was considered a requirement. He was correct from a strictly *Freudian* psychoanalytic perspective. But Sullivan had a different way of working, and he demonstrated that schizophrenics could form a transference and could be treated psychoanalytically. In fact, Sullivan's mentor, Edward Kempf, before him had demonstrated the same thing but got little recognition for it, except for Sullivan's later and somewhat quietly crediting him with that discovery. [18] Freud proved only that he was not effective in working with schizophrenics; after all, Freud was not God, in spite of what some of his followers thought. Sullivan, on the other hand, accumulated a promising track record with schizophrenics that brought him a certain fame. Of course, Sullivan had to discard some of Freud's paraphernalia to do so. The couch had to go, for example; a schizophrenic on a couch, if one could get him or her on a couch, would simply go to sleep. The other change Sullivan had to make in working therapeutically with psychotics was that he decided he had to talk when the patient would not. Freud, in his work with neurotics on the couch, could depend on the patient speaking eventually, if only out of anxiety, and perhaps even without the need to use the proverbial four-letter words. But Sullivan learned that sometimes with schizophrenics the therapist had to do all the talking until the patient was comfortable enough to venture a verbal contribution. Sometimes he failed to accomplish even that, and the treatment aborted.

Otto Kleinberg was one of the few prominent medical authorities who came under Sullivan's influence. He entered Sullivan's orbit in late 1931. He held degrees in both medicine and social psychology. Sapir was instrumental in luring Kleinberg into Sullivan's orbit. He was invited to sit in on seminars at Yale in which both Sapir and Sullivan promoted their views. Kleinberg later reported that he looked back on those early discussions as perhaps the most important beginning of his interest in the broad area of culture and personality, and thus influenced the field of anthropology. [19]

Freud's and Sullivan's long-term goals were also at some slight variance, but could be said to be complementary. Freud's goal was a healthy individual with an awareness that the unconscious is perpetually at work for good or for ill, potentially either undermining or edifying most anything. Persons who know that reality are, at very least, better prepared to face the exigencies of life. Sullivan's goals with patients did not contradict Freud's thesis but rather expanded it. For Sullivan, the patient's satisfactory social existence was the *sine qua non* of psychological health. Were Freud and Sullivan still available to us, they would certainly have agreed on their common purpose and philosophy of psychiatric treatment, even with their respective differences of focus and style; that is, the capacity both for work and love.

A large part of the variance between Freud and Sullivan stemmed from the extreme difference in their respective social origins. Freud was somewhat immunized from the disease of social isolation amidst his Jewish culture and his extensive family connections, carried forward by five offspring, a wife, a live-in sister-in-law who was also a mistress, and a nexus of various other relatives and members of the Jewish community coming and going. Sullivan's family was about as much of a reverse image of Freud's as one could construct. Sullivan was an only surviving child of an emotionally disturbed mother and a withdrawn, silent father, raised in a sparsely populated and impoverished rural area in central New York State. His early social life was almost entirely with chickens, cows, and horses. His childhood was one of extreme social isolation, his beloved Aunt Margaret and her visits from Brooklyn to see "her Harry"—who "twinkled"—being apparently a notable exception. [20] In maturity, he never had a family or children of his own, save for his adoption of a mentally disturbed teenage waif, James Inscoe, whom he housed and cared for the rest of his life, and whom he clearly loved and redeemed socially.

For both Freud and Sullivan, their social existence or lack thereof shaped their views of psychological health. That Freud decided to work mostly with neurotics and that Sullivan worked mostly with psychotics is quite understandable. They each elected to work with persons of their own kind. (Note that Sullivan's use of the male pronoun throughout was the custom in his generation and should not be taken as particular evidence of gender bias on his part beyond what bias was embedded in the culture at large.)

---

1. Boisen, Anton T. (1960). *Out of The Depths: An Autobiographical Study of Mental Disorder and Religious Experience.* New York: Harper & Brothers, Publishers, p. 9.

2. Boisen, Anton T. (1936). *The Exploration of the Inner World: A Study of Mental Disorder and Religious Experience.* Philadelphia: University of Pennsylvania Press, p. 1.

3. Clara Thompson, "Introduction", p. xxxiv, in Sullivan, Harry Stack. (1962). *Schizophrenia As a Human Process.* New York: W. W. Norton & Company, Inc.

4. Perry, Helen Swick. (1982). *Psychiatrist of America: The Life of Harry Stack Sullivan.* Cambridge, MA: The Belknap Press of Harvard University, p. 13.

5. Sullivan, *op. cit.*, p. xiii.

6. Lawrence, Raymond J. (1989). *The Poisoning of Eros: Sexual Values in Conflict.* New York: Augustine Moore Press, pp. 166–195.

7. Perry, *op. cit.*, pp. 421–2.

8. Evans, F. Barton III. (2006). *Harry Stack Sullivan: Interpersonal Theory and Psychotherapy.* New York: Routledge, Taylor and Francis Group; see also Jonathan Shedler. (2010). "The Efficacy of Psychodynamic Psychotherapy." *American Psychologist,* 65(2), pp. 98–109.

9. From Henry Nouwen's unpublished notes of his visit with Boisen in August 1964. Boisen, in decline but gracious and talkative, was housed in a room with no door, just off the Elgin Hospital refectory. He attributed his success largely to Freud's writings. Nouwen reported that Boisen had had another psychotic episode in the 1960s. No other visits with Boisen in the final year of his life are registered. Henri J. M. Nouwen Archives & Research Collection, John M. Kelly Library, University of St. Michael's College, 113 St. Joseph Street, Toronto, Ontario, Candada M5S 1J4..

10. Stokes, Allison. (1985). *Ministry After Freud.* New York: The Pilgrim Press, p. 177.

11. Stokes, *op. cit.*, p. 166.

12. Capps, Donald. (2008). *Jesus the Village Psychiatrist.* Westminster: John Knox Press.

13. Sullivan, Harry Stack. (1953). *The Interpersonal Theory of Psychiatry.* New York: W. W. Norton & Company Inc, New York, p. 15.

14. Ibid.,p. 13.

15. Sullivan, Harry Stack. (1962). *Schizophrenia as a Human Process.* New York: W. W. Norton & Company Inc., p. 9.

16. Blitsten, Dorothy R. (1953). *The Social Theories of Harry Stack Sullivan.* New York: The William-Frederick Press. p. 11.

17. Freud, Sigmund; James Strachey, trans. and ed. (1969). *The Question of Lay Analysis.* New York: The Norton Library, pp. 105–8.

18. Perry, *op. cit.*, p. 357; see also Edward J. Kempf. (1921). *Psychopathology.* St. Louis, MO: C.V. Mosey.

19. Otto Klineberg, quoted in Perry, *op. cit.*, p. 357.

20. Perry, *op. cit.*, p. 109.

CHAPTER 2

Sullivan: The First Thirty Years, 1892–1922

ᗯᗢᗯ

Harry Stack Sullivan was born in 1892 in Chenango County, central New York State, near but not in the remote village of Smyrna, which was at that time populated by about 300 persons. The nearest larger town was Norwich, twelve-and-a-half miles away. Since the depression of 1825 and the depression of 1894, the culture as well as the population of the area had declined. In 1900, Smyrna experienced a massive fire and was for the most part not subsequently rebuilt. In the twentieth century, its population continued to dwindle; by a third at the time that Swick Perry published her biography of Sullivan in 1982.

Chenango County itself is situated in what was referred to as the "Burned Over District." The metaphor alludes to the multiple religious revivals that circulated through the area in the early decades of the nineteenth century, in which so many people were saved so many times by so many religions, that there was no one left to be evangelized, thus "burned over." Chenango is the county where Joseph Smith and Brigham Young began their evangelical mission for the idiosyncratic new religion of Mormonism. But they were not the only evangelists at work in the area, *burning it over.*

Sullivan was born at a time when most transportation was horse-drawn. Railways were the most efficient method of travel as long as one was situated near a rail line, which Chenango County was not. Major roads and rail lines ran mostly east and west in the state, but the east-west lines were either north or south of Chenango. The most convenient rail station was about fifty miles north in Utica. The limitations of transportation had an isolating effect on the area. Roads were poor. Automobiles were just coming into being and the roads were not ready for them. Chenango County was the model for Theodore Dreiser's novel, *An American Tragedy*, published in 1925, when Sullivan was 33 years old.

Sullivan came up in what we would today consider extreme isolation, poverty, and social deprivation. There are no better words to describe Sullivan's childhood than "grimly isolating." He lived in the hills outside Smyrna. School was distant and in the winter often inaccessible. He was an only child who was reared by his grandmother when his mother temporarily disappeared without explanation when Sullivan was three. It is speculated that she attempted suicide and possibly was sent to a psychiatric hospital. The suicide rate for Chenango County was at that time at a ten-year high among all the rural counties in the state. [1]

Sullivan had access to only one neighborhood playmate, Clarence Bellinger, with whom he bonded at age eight-and-a-half. The two boys were quite different; Clarence was five years older, fat and born to a well-to-do but equally isolated Baptist family. Sullivan was small and skinny, though later gaining height, and born in relative poverty. The Sullivans were the rare Catholic family in the area, and the nearest Catholic Church was 12 miles away in Norwich. In spite of their five-year age difference and their class difference, their friendship seems to have survived through the high school years. In their rural sparsely populated rural countryside, neither boy had easy access to other boys or girls for peer relationships. But Sullivan's relationship with Bellinger was, according to Sullivan himself, a friendship that likely saved Sullivan's life, psychologically speaking. The relationship undoubtedly had much to do with Sullivan's later emphasis on relationships, particularly pre-adolescent relationships as essential to personality formation, and the key to understanding the workings of the human psyche. Their bonding seems to have set in motion Sullivan's (if not Bellinger's) subsequent view of life—namely, that human beings are nothing absent relationships with other human beings. [2]

Oddly enough, each became a notable psychiatrist. But in their professional journeys, Bellinger and Sullivan ultimately became bitter adversaries. The anthropologist Ruth Benedict also grew up in Chenango County. She and Sullivan became colleagues and were unique among Chenango natives in gaining international fame in that generation. Coincidentally, they spent part of the summer of 1948 together at a UNESCO conference in Czechoslovakia focused on "Childhood Education Towards World-Mindedness." It was to be the last summer for each of them; Benedict died that September on her return, and Sullivan the following January on his way home from yet another UNESCO meeting in Europe. Sullivan was scheduled to give Benedict's eulogy, but died before he was able to do so. [3]

Bellinger's professional zenith was to become the head of the Brooklyn Psychiatric Hospital. As Swick Perry characterized it, Bellinger became a big fish in a little pond, whereas Sullivan became a modest but sizable fish in the world at large. [4] Neither man married. In relation to their joint professions the two could hardly have moved farther apart. Sullivan was contemptuous of aggressive and physically manipulative psychiatric treatments, such as insulin, electro-shock therapy, and lobotomies, and publicly campaigned for the cessation of such abusive treatments. Bellinger was an early, continuing, and enthusiastic advocate of such treatment. Bellinger does not seem to have had devoted professional peers, whereas Sullivan had some weighty and significant ones, as well as a great many even more-weighty detractors. Unlike Bellinger, Sullivan became widely known in his field, both in this country and in Europe.

In addition to Bellinger, a bright light in Sullivan's childhood was his Aunt Margaret Stack, his mother's younger and more sophisticated sister who

27

never married. She had escaped Chenango County and eventually became a schoolteacher in Brooklyn. She took a special liking to her nephew. She liked to say that the Stacks "twinkled," and were charming. And that's the way she remembered "her Harry." Margaret is said to have been the kind of person who was never defeated. She gave her nephew what Myron Madden would call "her blessing." She came from a world far away from Chenango, and she kept "her Harry" supplied with a great many books from her life in The City; books he otherwise likely never would have had access to prior to college. [5]

Though very much a social isolate, Sullivan developed into a scholar. He triumphed in high school academically, if not socially, due certainly to his Brooklyn schoolteacher, Aunt Margaret, and her tutoring. He became valedictorian of his high school graduating class and the 1908 Chenango County recipient of a New York State scholarship to Cornell University. The state had a tradition of giving one such award in each county every year. (Perhaps it still does.) In late September of that year, Sullivan left Smyrna for Ithaca, only 50 miles to the west as the crow flies but much further by wagon and train, requiring a ride south, then west, then north, and finally west again. A horse-drawn conveyance traveling due west would have been a shorter route but would have taken more time and would have been a rough ride. A crow would have had a much shorter and more comfortable journey.

Sullivan seemed to have decompensated during that freshman year and at some point dropped out of college. He appeared not to have returned the following fall, or anytime thereafter. He may or may not have remained at Cornell for the full academic year. The accounts vary. Credible documentation is not available. And typical of Sullivan, he provides different accounts depending on to whom he was talking. At one point he stated that he stayed for a year and a half, but that is doubtful. His journey during the subsequent decade is at least foggy and almost impenetrable. He certainly never earned a bachelor's degree. Helen Swick Perry reported that he told her of having been hospitalized due to a schizophrenic break during that time. At some point by one account in 1911, he turned up enrolled at the Chicago College of Medicine and Surgery. Perry wrote that Sullivan implied to her that he had studied his own sickness at the medical college. Perry reported that the Editorial Committee of Sullivan's colleagues and friends, who sponsored the publication of his five volumes of writings, objected in 1961 to Perry's reporting that Sullivan had had at least one psychotic episode. But according to Perry, Sullivan confided in her that he had been hospitalized and was glad that he had not been subjected to electro-shock treatment or a lobotomy. [6] Perry also interviewed a colleague of Sullivan's, Kate Frankenthal, who said that Sullivan disclosed to her in 1947 that he had had "severe schizophrenic episodes" and Sullivan "still had them." [7]. According to Perry, Sullivan also published in the *American Journal of Psychiatry* (November 1929) the fact that he had been hospitalized in the fall of 1908. This has never been confirmed. [8]

❖ ❖ ❖

To skip ahead 30 years, in the autumn of 1939, Sullivan presented a series of five lectures consisting of the first of what was intended to be the annual series of the William Alanson White Memorial Lectures...a lecture series Sullivan himself established in honor of his late mentor. In the first lecture, he offered a remarkable description of an anonymous undergraduate's schizophrenic experience, which Perry assumed was an arm's length recounting of his own experience as a freshman at Cornell. [9]

"...a young man goes one night to the movies, alone, as usual. He often does this when he finds he cannot 'concentrate' on his studies— in which he is doing less and less satisfactory work. He often falls asleep over his books but even with nine or ten hours of sleep, he awakens less and less rested. Sleeping is becoming his major activity;

he can't seem to get enough of it. Yet he can't put the books aside and just go to bed; he knows he is not doing good work—and he is very ambitious to be a success. The movie is better than just chucking the book, and it is about the only thing he can do at night, except an occasional solitary walk. He has long since given up his efforts to be one of the boys, to play games and converse with others. They don't seem to find him interesting; in fact, some of them have made fun of him, quite openly. At least, he is pretty sure that that happened, and that none of them have much respect for him—but he does not think about that if he can help it.

"This particular evening, as the platinum-blonde heroine is revealed to the ecstatic audience in a moment of ingenuous helplessness, something happens to our boy. He has an 'electric' feeling; he is jolted out of his all too usual gloomy calm; he realizes that here is the Perfect Woman. He is 'in love.' He sits through a second showing of the film, aflame with mounting excitement. He goes out and walks the streets—walks, in fact, far out into the country. Dawn finds him writing a letter to his love. He may or may not mail it. If he does entrust it to the mailbox, in all likelihood the postman ultimately brings him a photograph—straight from Hollywood. But in any case, his life is changed. The gloom is gone. He is warmed by an inner fire. He spends long hours in fantasy about the dear one. Studies cease to have any relevance. And the people who were once sources of self-abasement, are now of no moment whatever.

"They wonder what happened to him; he does not notice them at all. The 'affair' may go on for months—as our boy moves on to the schizophrenic denouement. All the reality of the love-object is photographic. He has no need even for the sloppy 'details' of her life distributed to the hungry world in the movie journals. Everything is

30

provided by his revery processes; other people's view would garble his private perfection." [10]

Later, Sullivan followed with an account of the student's approach to a classmate:

"While he believes that he has become interested in a young lady, has sought her company and has finally got himself noticed so that he can discuss calculus with her, the facts which determine that situation are very much more on the side of the genital lust movie experience than they are on the intellectual pursuit of calculus. But it is only of the latter that he can be aware, and so he is constantly having difficulties in his interpersonal relations.

"The girl has regarded his 'approach' as quite subtle—but he never arrives. She may give him a helping hand, but he somehow overlooks or misinterprets it. If she makes the best of a bad job and they actually discuss calculus problems—even then as under any other circumstance—he leaves unsatisfied, with a feeling that things have not worked well. That night, he awakens wet with perspiration, from a dream in which he has been kissing and fondling this girl's breasts—and has just bitten one and swallowed the nipple!" [11]

Sullivan continued:

"If the person does not mature sexually by the time that person is seventeen years of age, then the disturbance can be so decompensating that "even internists talk about the late maturity type." [12]

In the next lecture, Sullivan noted that "the person who has not had the security of adequate preadolescent experience," as he is confronted with the appearance through maturation "of uncomplicated lust and the desirability of the genital organism," at the same time as the appearance of "obscure and warped...heterosexual interests, it is that person who develops psychosis." Perry suggested that Sullivan was writing about his own experience, his own feelings of inadequacy in his unequal experience with his only chum, Clarence. [13]

In his teaching of psychiatric residents Sullivan warned them to be skeptical of male patients who say, "I have never had any sexual interest in a woman except my mother"—and of women who speak similarly of their fathers. Sullivan concluded that such patients have had a history of tentative heterosexual desires that were rebuffed. The isolation in adolescence from an authentic chum is one of the most destructive of the manifestations of autoerotic arrest...leading to "a paranoid personality, if not to schizophrenia, and frequently suicide." [14] Again, Perry believed that Sullivan was describing his own history here, a quite plausible reading of the data.

❖ ❖ ❖

Subsequent to his aborted studies at Cornell University in the academic year 1908–9, Sullivan, at age 19, next appeared enrolled at Chicago College of Medicine and Surgery in 1911, without the benefit of an undergraduate degree. That in itself was not unusual. Sullivan's chum, Clarence Bellinger, himself went directly from high school to medical school. When the Chicago College requested Sullivan's transcript from Cornell, it received nothing. Where Sullivan had been in the intervening two years is not clear. He may have been a patient at Bellevue Hospital in Manhattan, treated by the then-principal Freudian in the country, A. A. Brill, who consulted there in 1908–1911. Brill and Sullivan certainly did ultimately connect personally, if not precisely at that time, and initially developed strong ties, which suggests that the presumption is correct. It is noteworthy that both Brill and Sullivan emphasized the signal importance of the hospital attendant, or nurse, in the recovery of schizophrenic patients, a conviction that may well have come from Sullivan's own experience as a psychiatric patient at Bellevue. It was certainly a principle that Sullivan put into practice later at Sheppard Pratt, the practice of training orderlies, nurses, and other non-physicians to function as lay psychotherapists, and a practice through which he became famous. Perry wrote that Sullivan made reference to his personal knowledge of institutional care as early as 1908, though Perry believed he probably meant 1909. Sullivan may have been telling us that he had been hospitalized either during or soon after his freshman year at Colgate. In any case, he seemed to be focused on understanding his own pathology while still even a teenager.

Sullivan left the Chicago College of Medicine and Surgery in 1915, ineligible for a degree. He also owed back fees. Chicago College then closed its doors as a consequence of the Flexner Report. It was sold first to Valparaiso and later to Loyola, neither of which seem to have a record of Sullivan's being awarded a medical degree. However, a diploma, properly signed and executed by Loyola in September 1917, was found in Sullivan's effects at his death. It was then forwarded to Loyola for their files. No one thus far claims to know what actually occurred regarding his graduation. [15]

The authenticity of the medical school diploma is therefore uncertain, but knowing Sullivan, a desperate young man, it could well have been forged. If fake, it was a noble and appropriate forgery. The diploma does show the first formal use of the name that Sullivan ultimately adopted: "Harry Stack Sullivan." The thin record of his academic life laid aside, what Sullivan ultimately accomplished in life is testimony to his learning and testimony as well to the dubious quality of formal education when compared with Sullivan's self-education. Considering the whole academic picture, we must conclude that Sullivan was essentially a self-educated man.

Between 1915 and 1921, Sullivan's doings are not entirely clear. There are conflicting stories. Records do show that he enlisted in the National

Guard in the First World War, and that he was discharged on November 7, 1916, because of some kind of physical disqualification. We would have to conjecture that the problem was psychological. In the following winter, it is said that he submitted to 75 hours of psychoanalysis, possibly, again, from A. A. Brill himself in New York City. There were no analysts in Chicago at that time. Perry reported that Sullivan was struggling during those years; struggling to find employment and, in Perry's judgment, bordering on schizophrenic panic. During that period, he did by some means form a lasting bond in Chicago with two notable sociologists, Robert Park and W. I. Thomas. By 1921, he was in Washington with a civil service job, which assigned him as a military liaison to St. Elizabeths Hospital.

When Sullivan left the Army after World War I, he tried several jobs that did not satisfy him. Finally, he received an appointment to the Federal Board of Vocational Education, a job that ended in November 1920. After some time in Chicago and Smyrna, taking care of his sick father, he received a telegram appointing him to St. Elizabeths Hospital in Washington, D.C., to be liaison officer for the Veterans Administration. There he fortuitously fell into the orbit of William Alanson White, arguably the preeminent psychiatrist in the country at the time, who took him under wing. [16]

When Sullivan died in Paris, his body was taken for a toxicological exam because of the uncertainly over the cause of death. Perry thought it ironic that toxicology was the only course in which he received an "A" at the Chicago College of Medicine and Surgery. [17]

❖ ❖ ❖

Some tangential cultural history is relevant to Sullivan's story. In that era, a cosmic shift was taking place in medical education. The so-called *Flexner Report* was published in 1911 after six years of intensive research, and Sullivan ran headlong into that turmoil through no fault of his own. Written by Abraham Flexner, M.D., the report, exposing the generally poor condition of medical education almost everywhere, was published after Flexner, over the course of six years, visited and evaluated each and every medical school in the country. When the research was begun in 1904, conducted entirely by Flexner himself and funded by the Carnegie Foundation, there were 160 medical schools in the U.S. Chicago itself harbored 14, according to Wikipedia. By the time the results and recommendations of the Flexner Report were implemented some years later, only 31 medical colleges remained standing nationally. About 80 percent of the nation's medical schools were closed voluntarily or by legislative edict. Medical training was extended from two years to at least four but for many specialties, even more. Physicians became scarcer *and richer.*

The number of physicians graduating annually was cut to fewer than half, from 4,400 to 2,000. And incidentally, in that era African-American physicians were required only to treat African-American patients, the latter of whom were considered to be carriers of diseases. The *Flexner Report*—and Flexner himself—was hard-core racist, even if Flexner was correct about the state of medical education.

❖ ❖ ❖

Thus, the record of Sullivan's life in the decade between his decompensation at Cornell and through the First World War consists of bits and pieces that do not always fit together. Perry wrote that there are clues that Sullivan also experienced another psychotic break during that period. But Sullivan's motto, she averred, was "always keep up appearances." Not a bad motto, actually. But it presents difficulties for biographers like Perry.

Perry also pointed out that Sullivan was willing to falsify data when it served his purposes (and, for what it's worth, Perry clearly loved the man). He changed his name and birth date more than once. Harry Francis Stack

Sullivan in high school later became H. F. Sullivan, and eventually H. Stack Sullivan, until finally, he went by Harry Stack Sullivan. He also changed his birth year from 1892 to 1886, giving himself six more years of maturity, and making himself one year older than his closest childhood friend and later adversary, Clarence Bellinger. He also very likely elongated his time at Cornell from one year—probably less—to one-and-a-half years.

Sullivan is reported by Perry to have been a professed lover of alcohol, who argued that the human race might owe its survival to the discovery of ethyl alcohol. Sullivan said he used alcohol as a way to deal with his own anxiety and for his angina as well. He acknowledged that he consumed annually an amount of spirits that would ruin the livers of most persons. [18] He also acknowledged that alcohol had its treacherous aspect. If Sullivan would qualify as an alcoholic—that is, addicted physiologically to alcohol— he was certainly a highly functioning alcoholic on the order of Winston Churchill. Sullivan's drink of choice was vodka with unsweetened grapefruit juice. After the evening meal, he regularly drank only 100-year-old French brandy. Perry wrote that she spent Christmas Eve with him in 1947, a year before he died. As the level of the brandy bottle went down, she saw no effect on his thinking. Previously, and usually, he had offered her a drink as well. This time, he did not. She wrote, "At age 54 [Perry was 35 at the time], I often saw in him the gaucheness of the shy young men whom I knew as an undergraduate." She had hoped, it seems, but to no avail, that he would have shared his brandy with her on that Christmas . [19]

The reader gets the feeling that, in addition to loving the man, Perry was sexually attracted to him as well, but probably to no avail. Perry also quoted a senior psychoanalyst colleague of hers who said that if Sullivan showed any interest, that she would gladly leave her husband and marry him. Sullivan never showed interest. [20]

1. Perry, Helen Swick. (1982). *Psychiatrist of America: The Life of Harry Stack Sullivan*. Cambridge: The Belknap Press of Harvard University Press.
2. Ibid., pp. 38–9, 119.
3. Ibid., pp. 76–81.
4. Ibid., p. 413.
5. Ibid., p. 315.
6. Ibid, pp. 104–117.
7. Ibid, pp. 3–4, 154.
8. Ibid., p. 337.
9. Ibid., p. 154.
10. Sullivan, CMP, p. 140 ff.
11. Perry, Ibid., p. 101; CMP, p. 68.
12. Ibid., 141–142. Quoting Harry Stack Sullivan, *Unpublished Lectures 7 & 8*, Washington School of Psychiatry 1943–44.
13. Sullivan, *Personal Psychopathology, op. cit.,* Ibid,. pp. 177–8.
14. Ibid., p. 417.
15. Perry, *op. cit.,* p. 335.
16. Ibid., p. 174.
17. Ibid., p. 18.
18. Ibid., p.174.
19. Ibid., p. 175.
20. Ibid., p. 335.

CHAPTER 3

Boisen's Beginnings

ᴄ∞ɔ

Anton T. Boisen was a both a Presbyterian and a Congregational minister, depending on the date. He had some doctrinal difficulties with both camps, as any rational person would. His ancestry was Danish-German on his father's side. His father immigrated to the U.S. in 1869. His mother's family, English and Irish, immigrated in the seventeenth century. Both parents were college teachers, from families of teachers. Boisen's father appears to have been erratic, high strung, often away on unexplained absences, with a difficulty holding jobs, but he was a man with a great deal of enthusiasm, and a lover of nature.

Boisen, born in 1876 in Bloomington, Indiana, was the first child of two; he had a younger sister. Both parents taught at some point at the University of Indiana. His father died of a heart attack at age 38 while teaching at Lawrenceville College in New Jersey, when little Boisen was six. His mother never remarried.

When Boisen was four, his mother discovered him playing with his genitals, and with her husband, rushed little Anton off to the doctor for an abrupt circumcision. In that era, circumcision was thought to be a preventative against masturbation. As Boisen himself put it,

"Quite spontaneously, it seemed, there had developed a sex-organ excitation which seemed beyond the normal. I can recall my parents' anxious concern and consultation with the doctor. He was sure it was due to local irritation, and the operation was performed. As a matter of fact, the trouble lay in a more than average interest in matters eliminative and sexual. Since it was thus primarily psychical, the treatment failed to correct it. The following summer, while at the home of my grandparents in Bloomington, this interest led to some mutual explorations with a boy cousin about a year younger. We were promptly caught and mouth was washed out with soap and water. This treatment seems to have put an end to the trend for the time being. The horror on my mother's face and her volunteered promise that she would not tell my father are impressions which still remain." [1]

Thus Boisen grew up—like most Americans of that era—with a profound and pathological bias against the libido in all its forms. For all the positive contributions he made to the world in his lifetime, he never recovered from an embedded and profound negativity toward sexual pleasure.

The Boisens were not alone in their views. At that time in late nineteenth-century America, there was a widely held belief that sexual self-pleasuring was both immoral and unhealthy, largely due to the influence of the likes of John Harvey Kellogg, M.D. (1852–1943), the breakfast cereal magnate, who went to extreme lengths to thwart masturbation, and in truth, sexual pleasure of any sort. Kellogg himself allegedly had a sexless marriage, with a separate bedroom for his wife, although they adopted seven children and housed many others who were orphans.

One procedure that Dr. Kellogg performed was to suture the penis to the testicles to prevent erections. Another was the application of carbolic acid to the clitoris in order to allay excitement. He also surgically removed the clitoris as a last resort. In his campaign against masturbation, Kellogg invented "Corn Flakes," which were alleged to assuage libidinal urges. Presumably, Corn Flakes were less nurturing to the libido than, say, bacon and eggs. (Kellogg's contemporary, Sylvester Graham, yet another late nineteenth-century warrior against the evils of sexual pleasure, created the "Graham Cracker," which also was alleged to lessen sexual arousal.)

Kellogg and his fellow travelers' negativity toward sexual pleasure of any sort permeated American culture and has prevailed even into the present era in some quarters. Boisen himself was a vivid clinical case exemplifying the influence of Kellogg and company.

At age eight, little Anton permanently lost his sight of one eye when he stood firm against neighbors' attempting to seize pears from his family's tree. When one of the intruders pointed a toy gun in his face, Boisen stood firm. He had recalled his grandfather saying that blinking was a defensive act, and he did not want to be defensive. So he refused to blink in the face of the gun. The gun was fired and made him blind in one eye. But the eyelid was untouched, suggesting that in fact he did not blink. Thus he proved his courage, but, for the rest of his 89-year life, he was a one-eyed man. His loss of vision never seemed to bother him. [2]

As the years passed from grade school to high school, Boisen's peers gradually changed their clothing appropriately. Instead of knickerbockers (now known as knickers), the boys began wearing more adult-style long pants. Boisen's mother forced him to remain in knickerbockers, keeping him dressed as a preadolescent against his wishes, seemingly, again, not wanting Boisen to grow up. [3]

After high school, Boisen enrolled at the University of Indiana, located in his hometown. He had trouble making a social adjustment in college. Two "good" fraternities "spiked him," as he put it, which seems to have meant he was blackballed. Boisen majored first in modern languages. But French literature presented continuing emotional turmoil for the sexually repressed, now adolescent Anton. On occasion, the stimulation of his libido from reading French novels would result in spontaneous orgasms, which humiliated this mama's boy.

Boisen was at least quite candid about the inner conflict he experienced in his efforts to be what he considered an ethical person in relation to sex. One day, to take a break from Tolstoy's erotic novel, *Anna Karenina,* he went outside to burn caterpillars from the mulberry tree in his yard. That involved a long pole with a piece of cloth soaked in kerosene tied to the end. To rid the tree of caterpillars, one lights the cloth and extends the pole up under the caterpillar nest. (I've done the same myself.) When Boisen was done with the chore, he put the pole back in the shed and went back to reading *Anna Karenina.* Soon he heard sirens coming closer to his home; looking outside to see about all the commotion, he saw his garden shed in flames. [4]

Boisen graduated from the University of Indiana in 1898 and was subsequently given an Advanced Instructorship in Romance languages at Bloomington High, while simultaneously continuing classes in French and German literature at the University in quest of a graduate degree. Before long, the pervasive sexual stimulation of French literature in particular drove him to the brink. As he put it, "They added fuel to the fire that was already more than I could control." He became alarmed when certain sexually oriented words in his Greek dictionary leaped off the page and hit him in his one good eye. Boisen labeled them "obscene." At least he was savvy enough to become alarmed, realizing that his problems with sex were serious. By age 21, sexual issues increasingly vexed him. Then something seemed to say to him, "Don't be afraid to tell." So, he followed that inspiration and talked to his *mother,* without a doubt the worst possible choice of a confidant for an adult male needing help with his libidinal conflict, and in particular, this mother.

Rather than test fate further, Boisen confronted his "unassimilated sex problem" by leaving the study of and teaching of romance languages, and entered forestry school. After completing his studies there, he got a job with the forest service. Trees do not portray acts of fornication; Boisen could relax for a while. [5]

In 1902 Boisen met Alice Batchelder, who had come to Indiana University as secretary of the Young Women's Christian Association. It was love at first sight for Boisen, and what followed was a one-sided and abusive love affair that lasted for 33 years. Boisen took the abuse as if he deserved it. After his attempt to contact her following her visit, her first response was that the relationship should cease entirely. In desperation, Boisen resorted to opening the Bible and reading random passages for guidance. The first was "ask and you shall receive...." He kept asking for 33 years and apparently never got so much as a kiss. Boisen's next-attempted random openings of the Bible for answers was, "Behold thy mother," which Boisen somehow interpreted as a message to continue pursuing Alice. [6]

Through the subsequent decades, Alice relayed a string of no's, very few yes's or maybe's, and an occasional and very misleading "come and get it," but mostly—by far—the former. Boisen remained the perpetual supplicant. But his discovery of Alice led Boisen to go into the ministry, likely thinking that this pious, seemingly asexual woman would find him more appealing as a cleric. To some extent it did the trick; she actually consented to see him at a religious meeting in Philadelphia in early winter 1908. At the end of the meeting, she offered her hand, which Boisen kissed, and the words of her enigmatic response were, "God's promises always come true." [7] That, of course, gave him hope. Following the meeting, he wrote her, pursuing the relationship. Alice replied that he must have misunderstood, that her first answer had been final and could not be changed. By now, Boisen must have been an emotional wreck. He was committed to a schizophrenigenic woman, a carbon copy of his mother, if ever there was one.

In fall of 1908, Boisen nevertheless enrolled at Union Theological Seminary in New York City. He was disappointed to find no courses there in psychology. Being fully aware that he had psychological problems, he wanted to learn more about himself and his problems. He petitioned the dean for such a course, and his petition was answered. A course in "the Psychology of Religion" was instituted, but that also disappointed him. He wanted something that might help him understand his own pathology. He was aware that he would not likely find what he sought in such a class. During the seminary years, however, he felt that he had won, for the time being, his continuing battle for "self-control," obviously a reference to his efforts to restrain from masturbation and spontaneous ejaculation.

During Christmas 2010, Alice visited Boisen at the seminary, saying that she had decided to give her heart a chance, continuing her whiplash posture in relation to Boisen's attempt to court her. After Alice departed, Boisen's roommate opined that Alice "did not show the kind of love" for Boisen that he would have wished to see, likely meaning that he saw no evidence of Alice's libido in relation to Boisen.

Undaunted, Boisen arranged a later visit with Alice. She agreed to a rendezvous, but showed up in the company of a woman companion. From Boisen's perspective, the rendezvous was aborted with Alice's creation of the threesome...which undoubtedly was Alice's intent.

Boisen graduated from seminary in 1911. Unable to find a pastorate at first, he took on a temporary job doing pastoral survey work in Missouri. Next, he took a pastorate in a country church in Kansas. After receiving the appointment, Boisen wrote Alice suggesting that she join him as a pastor's wife. Her response was a vigorous and contemptuous "no." After two years, he left the position, feeling like a failure. Following that, he took a position at a church in Maine, with desultory results. Still, he persevered with his postal romancing of Alice.

Then came World War I, "the Great War." Boisen signed up as a Secretary with the Overseas Young Men's Christian Association and was one of the first Americans to be sent to France, arriving there in September 1917. After the armistice in 1918, Boisen spent six months in Germany. Sigmund

Freud was not far away, in Vienna, desperate for British and American currency. Undoubtedly, Freud would have taken Boisen into treatment had the opportunity presented itself. But Boisen likely had learned nothing about Freud from his Psychology of Religion course at Union. Quite ironically, reading Freud a year later radically changed Boisen's life and ultimately altered the character of American Protestantism—and later, other manifestations of religion as well—for the better.

Boisen returned home in July 1919. He had, of course, been thinking of Alice throughout his time in Europe. On arrival home, he just "had to see her." She was working at this time in a bank in Chicago. So, he traveled to see her, but she adamantly refused to receive him. Returning home, he wrote her but received no reply. Then in June 1920, Alice wrote, inviting him to visit her. Thus, he traveled back to Chicago and was invited to dinner at her apartment. When he arrived, he was chagrined to discover two "maiden ladies" as additional guests. Of course there was no opportunity to talk privately. Once again, Boisen was thwarted in his efforts to court Alice. She later summed up the dinner meeting by letter saying that her first answer, long ago had been final. Alice should have at least reimbursed him for one of the two train tickets to Chicago, if not both. [8]

On October 9, 1920, Boisen had his first really significant psychotic break. A cadre of police and physicians came to his home, restrained him, and took him to the Psychopathic Hospital for lockup. During the first week of his psychiatric incarceration, he was violent and severely out of control and, of course, was restrained and drugged. At the end of that brief period, he was back to his old self. On October 16, having snapped out of his delirium, Boisen was transferred to Westboro Hospital, where he seemed to have remained cooperative until his release in late January 1922, an involuntary incarceration period of about 16 months. During that time, he was cooperative with the hospital regimen, although he felt considerable contempt for the ill-informed physicians treating him. On Boisen's arrival at

Westboro, his life-long seminary friend Fred Eastman brought him a copy of Freud's newly published *Introductory Lectures.* The book captured Boisen's imagination and changed his life. He was a Freudian from that point on, feeling that the book spoke directly to his own difficulties. As indeed it did.

Inspired by Freud, Boisen decided that he must create a clinical training program for clergy, promoting a method for them to work both pastorally and therapeutically with psychiatric patients like himself. From that vision, Boisen went on to change the nature of pastoral training. He went on to redefine the therapeutic task of the pastor and other religious professionals in the twentieth century, establishing the task of the pastor as psychotherapist, and thus changed the terms of the debate. The irony here is that Boisen envisioned the possibility of psychiatric healing and the role in that healing that religious professionals might play. But somehow Boisen never quite received that healing for himself. *He saved others; himself he could not save.* [9]

Though diagnosed as schizophrenic—a diagnosis that he never actually entirely escaped from his entire life—he made good use of both his hospitalization and his illness. For the rest of his life, between his five or six psychotic episodes, Boisen was quite rational, productive, and in fact often brilliant. Contrariwise, he did not make good use of the hospital physicians. They tried to tell him that his sexual standards were rigid and too high, and they were neurotic and dangerous to his mental health. And of course they were correct, but Boisen held their externalistic advice in contempt. Seemingly the physicians had never read Freud. Boisen sought no behavioral advice from physicians or anyone else; he sought only psychotherapy.

At about midpoint during his Westboro hospitalization, Boisen began lobbying for a transfer to Bloomingdale Hospital in New York, where it was reported that the staff was using the Freudian approach to treatment. Boisen argued that there, he would able "to observe its effectiveness." His choice of words was telling, indicating his intention to merely put a toe in the Freudian water. However, a transfer was scheduled. The night before the scheduled transfer, Boisen suffered a brief relapse. We should understand this as evidence of Boisen's ambivalence. He believed that Freud's approach was effective, and remarkably, his thinking had been radically altered in reading Freud's *Introductory Lectures*; but at the time, Boisen was not entirely sure that he wanted the treatment for himself.

On release from the hospital in early 1922, Boisen went immediately to Harvard with the intention of preparing himself to work on the task of addressing psychological problems with other clergy like himself. He was on a personal mission to bring clergy to an understanding of mental illness, and ways to address it clinically and therapeutically, profoundly informed as he was by his own personal experience, and inspired from reading Freud's *Introductory Lectures*. He established a close relationship with the well-known physician, Richard Cabot, the creator of medical social work. Cabot and Boisen bonded quickly. From Cabot, Boisen learned his clinical method. Inspired by Freud, and with tools in hand, he envisioned training other clergy in applying this method in their work with troubled persons. Cabot supported Boisen intellectually, morally, and also financially for the subsequent seven years. It was a fortuitous relationship; without Cabot's support, one wonders whether Boisen would have been able to accomplish much of anything on his own. During 1923 and 1924, Boisen took a job in the Social Service Department at Boston Psychopathic Hospital, where he learned how to work with psychiatric patients. He continued to take classes under Cabot at Harvard, and Cabot continued to support him morally and financially. Professor Arthur Holt of Chicago Theological Seminary also supported Boisen's ambitions.

Cabot had some contact with the Superintendent of Worcester State Hospital, Dr. William A. Brian, who was willing to hire Boisen for the position of Chaplain at Worcester State. Thus on July 1, 1924, Boisen began his improbable position as staff chaplain in a public psychiatric institution, barely two-and-a-half years after he himself was sprung from an involuntary psychiatric incarceration in a similar institution. (This must be one of the most astonishing reversals in psychiatric hospital history.)

Superintendent Brian was not particularly religious. But when the local morning newspaper in glaring type proclaimed, "Local Hospital Appoints Soul Healer," Dr. Brian countered this public ridicule, stating, "I would appoint a horse doctor if I thought it would help my patients." Boisen was chagrined at such publicity and, as a result, made it his personal policy assiduously to avoid newspapers and magazines; he would stick with scientific journals thereafter. [10]

Boisen went to work immediately to create a program for chaplain interns, with the purpose of training ministers to work therapeutically and pastorally with mentally disturbed persons. In less than a year, he inaugurated his first clinical pastoral training group for the summer of 1925, enrolling a group of four interns. In the first years, these pastors-in-training were hired by the hospital as half-time orderlies, not chaplains. The design was for the chaplain-trainees to learn as orderlies how to relate to psychologically disturbed patients as persons and to gather clinical data during the day. In the evening, they shared their assessments in clinical pastoral seminars. This design also provided some income for the trainees. Boisen's notion was that ministers needed first to learn how to communicate and relate to psychiatrically disturbed persons, and that the assumption of a religious role at the beginning of a relationship with a patient would be counter-productive and impede that learning. [11] In retrospect, this may have been a more productive design than what subsequently followed in later years, when trainees became universally identified by title as "Chaplain Interns," giving patients the initial impression that the chaplain had come to do something *religious,* thus circumventing the clinical posture.

Boisen's new training regimen quickly morphed into a nationwide movement, and later a world-wide movement, involving some hundreds of hospitals that established similar training programs, revolutionizing the Protestant ministry in the U.S. in the 1930s—and later, almost all forms of pastoral ministry in this country and beyond. As clergy learned how to relate therapeutically to patients by way of clinical case studies (as opposed to their typical role as "teachers of religion" and "prayer warriors"), they became listeners and pastoral psychotherapists.

Boisen was not simply a recovering, but episodic, crazy man who found a job. He was a curious, amazingly well-read person who diligently sought to understand his own predicament as a sometime-psychotic and at the same time sought to reach out to others in similar straits. In that era—and to a large extent, still today—mentally disturbed persons were simply warehoused until they died. In his efforts to wage war against that social policy, Boisen read everything he could find on the matter in books and journals of psychiatry, sociology, and anthropology. In his first year at Worcester State, Boisen came across what was the very first journal article from the pen of Harry Stack Sullivan, a newly minted psychiatrist and psychoanalyst at Sheppard and Enoch Pratt Hospital in Townsend, Maryland, near Baltimore. Boisen wrote, "I chanced upon Harry Stack Sullivan's 'Conservative and Malignant Features of Schizophrenia' in the *American Journal of Psychiatry,* July, 1924." Boisen continued, "I was deeply interested in this paper, for it gave needed support to my own views." [12]

Newly out of psychiatric confinement, Boisen wrote to Sullivan directly about the paper, and Sullivan responded by inviting him to come visit him at Sheppard Pratt. Boisen made the trip, but there is no available data as to what transpired during that visit. However, what followed was a 25-year friendship of two colleagues, Sullivan and Boisen, who ultimately and radically altered their respective disciplines, psychotherapy and pastoral training, almost singlehandedly.

The tragic irony in the life mission of Boisen was that he never actually came to a clear understanding of his own psychiatric problems in any depth.

After his Westboro hospitalization, the sometime-psychotic clergyman revolutionized pastoral work but experienced at least four subsequent psychotic breaks over the course of his long life. All were brief episodes, and he recovered from them quickly; but while Boisen helped to cure many, he could not cure himself.

---

1.   Boisen, Anton T. *Out of the Depths: An Autobiographical Study of Mental Disorder and Religious Experience*, New York: Harper & Brothers, Publishers, 1960, p. 9.
2.   Boisen, *op. cit.*, pp. 30–31.
3.   Ibid., p. 35.
4.   Ibid., pp. 44.
5.   Ibid., pp. 44–50.
6.   Ibid., p. 55.
7.   Ibid., p 58.
8.   Ibid., p. 73.
9.   A paraphrase of "The Gospel of Matthew", Chapter 27, verse 42, *The New English Bible: The New Testament*, Oxford University Press, 1970, p. 41.
10. Boisen, *op. cit.*, p. 151.
11. Ibid., p. 151.
12. Ibid., p. 156.

CHAPTER 4

The Idiosyncratic Sullivan

∽∽∽

The fastest route, and the most reliable, toward understanding Harry Stack Sullivan as a person—or even as a psychotherapist and psychoanalyst—is through the pages of Helen Swick Perry's *Psychiatrist of America: The Life of Harry Stack Sullivan*. [1] This is the only thoroughgoing biography of Sullivan in existence and will likely hold that status permanently. For a grasp of Sullivan's ideas and theories, there are numerous additional and complementary sources. The two other most accessible and useful sources known to me are *Harry Stack Sullivan: Interpersonal Theory and Psychotherapy* by F. Barton Evans III; [2] and *The Social Theories of Harry Stack Sullivan* by Dorothy R. Blitsten. [3] Evans and Blitsten detail how Sullivan worked as a psychiatrist, and are less about biography. And of course the two monographs that he wrote in his lifetime, and the five collections of his papers are revelatory, but do not reveal much about his personal life.

Helen Swick Perry began working for Sullivan as a secretary in 1946 and had close and personal access to him during the last three years of his life. She was awed by his character, knowledge, and prestige. She apparently gave Sullivan no indication that she might write his biography, and that was almost certainly not part of her job description, nor likely even on her mind. But she did, and history should credit her. It is a vivid work, written out of love and admiration—and plentiful documentation. We can have no assurance that she got every detail correct, or that she was perfectly candid in every respect, but she is apparently the only person in history who worked with Sullivan up close over the last three years of his life—and who had a grasp of who he was as a person and what he did for a living during those years. She was his secretary, and she turned out to be a splendid choice. She published the biography in 1982, an astonishing 33 years after his death. Her work has been criticized by some, but in my view it stands up well to criticism. Whatever bias she may have had—and who is without bias?—she had something that no one else had who was willing to talk: a very close association with Sullivan during the last years of his life.

At the time of his death in 1949, Sullivan had published only one book, *Conceptions of Modern Psychiatry*, in 1947. [4] He had, however, published countless journal articles and lectures. He had also written *Personal Psychopathology* [5] sometime between 1929 and 1933, but he withheld it from the public, sharing it privately with select persons.

There may be many millions of Sullivan's words preserved in one form or another, but most of the collection is very difficult to access. He had founded the journal *Psychiatry,* still publishing today, in 1938. He was its editor for the decade prior to his death, meaning, of course, that he could publish his views at will. Thus Sullivan's written work was in some fashion quite public, though a tad under the radar, and therefore not readily accessible to the public. Ordering a book may be easy, but getting one's hands on a specific journal article, especially in that era, was usually a more complicated and expensive task, and in fact still is, even now in the cyber age. Furthermore, there are countless hours of recordings of Sullivan's lectures and consultations presented at Chestnut Lodge in Towson, Maryland, and elsewhere, most of which likely have never been listened to since.

Subsequent to Sullivan's death in 1949, Perry became something of a point person and editor in a group effort inaugurated by Sullivan's closest colleagues, whose mission was to preserve Sullivan's widely disbursed writings. David McKenzie Rioch seems to have been central to that project. Others listed as involved were Clara Thompson, Otto Allen Will, Mabel Blake Cohen, Dexter M. Bullard, and Janet MacKenzie Rioch, psychiatrists all, and all devoted to Sullivan. They made up a sort of Sullivan recovery team, with access to a massive amount of published articles, much of the material redundant. They published only a fraction of it, making up five volumes consisting of about 2,500 pages of what they considered most valuable. In the first three collections, Perry is named as the principal editor. In the last two, she is recognized as providing "Introduction and Commentary." Perhaps by that time, the editing was done by the entire team.

The editorial team did not attempt to correct or modify Sullivan's own words or style, except in rare cases of blatant error or gross repetition, but published them as they found them. Sullivan's writing was often inscrutable, his writing style not amongst the most accessible examples of English usage in history, to state it generously. He was a healer, but without much real command of syntax or ability to communicate in writing. Or perhaps he was being deliberately subversive to English as the unrepentant Irishman that he was. Sometimes, he failed to demonstrate that he knew the value of punctuation; there is at least one sentence of his that well surpassed 150 words in length.

Perry died in 2001, at the age of 90, eventually became a psychiatric authority in her own right, and spent her latter years on the staff of the Langley Porter Psychiatric Institute in San Francisco. She published an analysis of the hippie phenomenon entitled *The Human Be-In.* Her biography of Sullivan is a compelling read, and has no rival. She was introduced to Sullivan by Donald Reeve, an autodidact printer at the Lord Baltimore Press who lacked a high school education. Beginning in 1937, Reeve had shepherded the publication of Sullivan's journal *Psychiatry,* even through its period of insolvency a decade later. Reeve considered Sullivan a charming man with delightful eccentricities. Perry wrote that Sullivan treated this uneducated man with unfailing respect, according him the stature of an expert in his own field. [6]

Any attempt to summarize Sullivan's theory of psychotherapy and psychoanalysis, which is embedded in his monumental collection of writings and recordings, is a Herculean task. Perry was never more correct than when she classified Freud as a Talmudic-style writer, with orderly and clear syntax, and Sullivan as a Joycean writer who wandered all over the page, seemed to contradict himself, and obfuscated as often as he discoursed with brilliance on a particular subject. (I say all this as an excuse for appearing disorganized myself as I attempt to explicate Sullivan's basic philosophy and his approach to psychotherapy.)

The classical psychiatrists—Kraepelin, Freud, and Jung—oriented their insights mostly to the individual and his or her psychological makeup. Sullivan, on the other hand, focused on the individual in the context of his or her relationships, the arena of the interpersonal and the social. He even went so far as to propose that individual identity is itself an illusion, entirely dependent on relationships with other human beings. Sullivan added that since psychiatry deals with living and everybody has a great deal of experience in living, that it is not very easy to develop a type of objectivity about the subject matter of psychotherapy.

Sullivan took the developmental approach. Some psychiatrists, said Sullivan, have had a great deal of training in treating persons who are ill, as if they were museum pieces to be examined in fine detail. In no other field of endeavor is the presumed authority's preconceptions as troublesome as in psychiatry, he asserted. The fabulous difficulty of teaching psychiatry, said Sullivan, is that it is extremely difficult to get any two people to mean just the same thing when they are engaged in a discussion about what they have supposedly learned in treating patients psychotherapeutically.

In his *Interpersonal Theory of Psychiatry,* Sullivan proposed three definitions of psychiatry. First, he said, was the broadest definition, "that confounding conglomerate of ideas and impressions, of magic, mysticism, and information, of conceits and vagaries, of conceptions and misconceptions, and of empty verbalisms." The second definition, which Sullivan called "the polite definition of psychiatry for the prescientific era [is] the art of observing and perhaps influencing the course of mental disorders." The third definition, which he said was the one he subscribed to, is that psychiatry "...is concerned with the kinds of events or processes in which the psychiatrist participates while being an observant psychiatrist [and]...consists of the actions or operations from which the psychiatric information is derived (and)...are events in interpersonal fields which include the psychiatrist [himself] and... consists of events in which the psychiatrist participates; and they are not events which he looks at from atop ivory towers." [7]

This summary is a condensation of about 360 tortuous and convoluted lines and phrases, which in their original are a stunning display of Sullivan's dreadful writing style. And yet, he makes his point.

For Sullivan, the psychiatrist's role was to try to "get something to happen," which he recognized that for florid schizophrenics was neither an easy task nor one that is assured of success. To that end, it is useful, he said, to have the patient prepare a chronology of his life. The therapist cannot expect a deeply disturbed patient to give up his shadowy vestiges of security by owning his psychosis, but even so, the psychiatrist should be asking the patient for something. He has to have something to work with until something more worthy comes along. That, according to Sullivan, is the whole story of intensive psychotherapy.

Sullivan mocked the use of the couch, and by implication, Freud as well, but playfully so. He claimed to have employed the couch in earlier times. "Come in, lie down on the couch and say every littlest thing that comes to your mind." Some patients could spend six months trying to relax completely, contended Sullivan. On the couch, Sullivan said, only those Anglo-Saxon words come to mind, words that one cannot say.

Sullivan thus gave up on the couch. He thought psychotherapy governed by free association would likely have to be measured in decades. Sullivan wanted to get something to happen between the patient and himself, then and there. This was a jab at Freud of course. But it was actually Sullivan's attempt to acquit himself against the master, and a master who declined to work with schizophrenics, considering them incurable. It would have been enough for him to say he was a different kind of therapist, working with radically different types of patients, with different objectives.

Unlike Freud, Sullivan worked from the beginning mainly with schizophrenic patients who require a different posture on the part of the therapist. With Freud dead or in serious decline, and Sullivan professionally alone in the world with few allies, he was likely attempting to show how his idiosyncratic method was legitimate in relation to the master. However, the reader should not assume that Sullivan was an opponent of Freud. Sullivan had a history of being quite abrupt with those close to him, and with those to whom he was indebted, and of contradicting himself at will, and often. He seemed to understand that the truth itself is at times contradictory.

From Sullivan's perspective, everyone coming to a therapist is busily interpreting the therapist while the therapist is similarly busy interpreting the client. Thus, there is no such thing as an "objective" observation. Subjectivity is inescapable, unlike in other forms of medical practice. The inevitable first task of the therapist is to communicate that he, too, is a human being. Furthermore, the therapist, to some degree, must communicate to the patient how he himself is doing. Otherwise the patient—especially a schizophrenic— is apt to be reduced to mutism. And to clumsily puncture the patient's self- esteem need not be fatal, provided the therapist learns from it and there is time left to do some reparation work. Anger directed at the patient, either in mild or severe form, is out of the question and should be understood as anxiety on the part of the therapist, which will be unproductive.

❖ ❖ ❖

Sullivan took issue with Melanie Klein and later Edith Jacobson and their contention that infants experience complex interactions between themselves and the object world of good and bad mothers. Sullivan's view, according to F. Barton Evans III, was that such complex experiences resided primarily in the mind of the psychoanalysts themselves, not the infant. Again, according to Evans, Sullivan argued that infants do not experience complex interaction between self and the object world of good and bad mothers. Their relationship needs are fairly simple and obvious. [8]

Sullivan followed Freud in attending to psychological stages of development in persons, beginning with the oral, anal, and phallic stages, which laid the foundation for describing the developmental patterns of behavior in persons. Erik Erikson's work also famously built on that premise. Without dismissing either Erikson or Freud, Sullivan on the other hand focused principally on the so-called latency stage, or pre-puberty, as in his view is the watershed and critical transition period of personality development. It would appear that both Sullivan and Freud were guided by their own particular human experience. After all, by what else can anyone be guided?

Sullivan was an only child in a family of three; two prior siblings had died in infancy. He lived with his mother and father in a fairly desolate rural area, far from school and from any convenient wider social opportunities. According to family values, his mother had "married down" socially. She also seemed to have disappeared for several years when Sullivan was a toddler, and his grandmother filled in as a substitute. Speculation was that she was hospitalized for psychiatric issues.

Freud was born into a radically different context. Multiple relationships within extended families and the Jewish subgroup were a given in his eastern European Jewish urban community. The young Freud was under no pressure to seek human contact in the form of a peer. This context was likely what *made* Freud, in stark contrast to the isolated, rural atmosphere of Sullivan's early years. Freud's and Sullivan's respective origins likely determined the kind of therapy they each embraced. As is widely known, Freud sought to examine the repressed and forgotten things in the soul/psyche. He sought dreams and the hidden and lost memories, and sought to reconcile the hidden with the known. Sullivan never viewed Freud's posture as wrong for neurotics, but both he and Freud concurred that such a therapeutic approach failed to be effective with schizophrenics.

Like Freud, Sullivan seemed to build his theory on his own experience. Preadolescence, therefore, represented for Sullivan a critical opportunity, at approximately age eight, for a first significant experience of peership, in the form of what he idiosyncratically labeled a "chum." His first friend, Clarence Bellinger, was 13 years old when they met, and apparently the only other near-peer within accessible distance. Despite their age difference, the two boys bonded, and for the first time, Sullivan, by his own account, felt he was a person. That experience shaped his view of psychosexual development forever after. We do not know much in the way of details about the relationship, except for Sullivan's claim that his first peer relationship was salvific for him. Nor do we know how long the friendship lasted. By the time Bellinger reached puberty, his relationship with Sullivan would have presumably changed. In spite of their five-year difference in ages, Bellinger left for college only two years ahead of Sullivan, who himself went off to Cornell in 1908 at age sixteen, with the coveted New York State scholarship in hand. In any case, the *chum* relationship, as Sullivan labeled it, was a watershed event in Sullivan's life and became a critical marker in his theory of human development.

There is no indication that the two had any further contact after those early school years, and no data seems to be available pertaining to when and how they became radically estranged. Although they both became psychiatrists, their respective therapeutic philosophies were about as oppositional as they could have been. In adulthood, the sparse data suggests that they seemed not to communicate personally.

Undoubtedly drawing from his own personal experience, Sullivan built his therapeutic theory and practice on the necessity of one finding positive relationships in preadolescence outside the boundaries of the family. A satisfactory interpersonal relationship was for Sullivan the *sine qua non* of mental health, a non-negotiable in Sullivan's theory, and on that theory he built his practice. His first real "practice" was his eight years at Sheppard Pratt, administering his own protected and isolated therapeutic ward consisting of his own handpicked staff, and personally selected patients as well. "The object was to create an environment in which the patient could pull himself together," wrote Sullivan. While other hospitals were still using psychotropic drugs, electro-shock, and lobotomies (the "icepick in the brain treatment as Sulivan called it), all with poor results, Sullivan was getting an 86% cure rate (some say 80%) with diagnosed schizophrenic patients. [9]

Sullivan saw that in psychosis the repressed and forgotten things were out in the open, exposed and running wild, though typically disguised. With psychotics, one need not go looking for what is hidden in the unconscious. It was as if the unconscious had spilled everything out in the open, even if in garbled terms. However, the eccentric and dissociative behavior of the psychotic, as Sullivan discovered, is typically revelatory. The therapist's burden is to read, or rather, to decipher what is being revealed in the bizarre behavior. Or, as Sullivan's mentor, William Alanson White said often, the psychiatrist's task is to discover what the patient is trying to do in his dissociative behavior.

Freud compared psychoanalysis with archeology, unearthing deeply buried remnants of the past and relating those remnants to the accessible present. Though Sullivan never said as much, he had no need to dig up deeply buried remnants of the soul. The broken pieces of the patient's soul were already laid out before him in the odd language and disjunctive behavior of the schizophrenic. Sullivan's way of working was like reading a new idiosyncratic language and attending to the nature of the human psyche, using whatever intelligible scraps were available. [10]

A significant difference between Freud and Sullivan was in the manner in which each engaged patients. In the Freudian stance, the therapist or analyst took the position of a listening consultant and did not typically take the initiative in promoting disclosure, behavioral goals, or directions. The therapist did not play the role of interlocutor and generally was not an actor in determining therapeutic results. Freud's stated role was to listen and ultimately to offer interpretations or connections if he had any. Freud had altered his earlier practice of using hypnosis as an instrument for bypassing the conscious mind and altering behavior, a treatment that he found not to have lasting results. As he moved from the approach of suggestion and hypnosis to analysis, he took on a radically revised posture. He left the patient to work out his own salvation, so to speak, using discoveries from analysis as he was able. This revised therapeutic posture worked well, and still works well with normal neurotics. But Sullivan elected to work with an entirely different type of clientele or patient, namely schizophrenics, and it is no wonder that Freud considered them untreatable. Indeed they were with respect to the accepted procedures of psychoanalysis. One must have a strong functioning personality, or ego, to endure and make good use of Freud's psychoanalysis. Schizophrenics have anything but a functioning ego.

Thus, Sullivan figured out how to work psychotherapeutically with psychotics and became remarkably successful at it, making a world-class reputation for himself. He discovered that his first task was to communicate; to make contact with the patient. Successfully making contact, or communicating, is not a foregone conclusion with any particular schizophrenic. They may elect to remain in their imaginary and delusional world, untouched and incommunicado. In this work, Sullivan had the advantage over Freud. He had been there himself, perhaps more than once, and was able to write about what a psychosis is like. The contextual world is irrelevant to a person in a psychotic state. He or she lives in a self-contained cocoon, impervious to the world around. Therefore, the first task for anyone attempting to work with a person in the midst of psychosis is to make interpersonal contact. This new posture involved engaging the patient actively, sometimes even speaking for the patient until the patient can speak for himself. And of course, sometimes Sullivan failed in making contact, in which case, the patient typically lived the rest of his life in the back wards of a psychiatric hospital.

Subsequent to his death Sullivan was assigned the label of an "ego psychiatrist," which seems an unfruitful category. I doubt he would have tolerated such a label while he lived; it would have been just as appropriate to label him an "id" psychiatrist, because he worked principally with patients whose ids were exposed, out in the open, and, in their decompensation, their actions difficult to fathom. The label "ego psychiatrist" may have been intended to distinguish Sullivan and Freud, and the way in which they each worked, but it falls short. Freud focused mostly on the id and the superego, and on how the two arenas affected the personality, or the ego. But Freud worked only with neurotics. Sullivan, by contrast, worked mainly with schizophrenics, whose egos were malfunctioning; his task, within the Freudian construct, was to restore the ego, if that could be accomplished. Restoring the ego meant learning to read both the superego and id, and holding them at bay, at least for a space of time. But in fact, Sullivan did not much employ Freudian language or constructs. While he read and studied Freud, and was clearly and admittedly indebted to him, Sullivan struck out on his own course. More to the point, Sullivan might properly be labeled "the psychiatrist for adolescents and for schizophrenics." (And we must note, in this context, William Silverberg's contention, supported by Sullivan, that ego, superego, and id are simply ways of being, not discrete things that can be identified or named.) [11]

❖ ❖ ❖

Sullivan did not overturn Freud by any means, but rather built on him. He expanded the Freudian vision by adding the *interpersonal* to the Freud's *intrapsychic*. Sullivan thus radically altered psychiatry in his brief lifetime. All psychiatry after him bears his strong imprint. Ego psychology, object relations, attachment theory, intersubjectivity, and so forth: all of the significant current trends and mini-movements in psychotherapeutic and psychoanalytic theory and practice subsequent to 1930 seem to be children of Sullivan, with no acknowledgement of paternity. Each of them has branched out from the Freudian focus on the individual, and the unconscious, to a focus on the nature of the interpersonal relationships of the particular individual. And this transition is not a diminution of Freud in any way. It is building on what Freud originally built, with its strong scaffolding.

At one point, when working with the anthropologist Edward Sapir, Sullivan described himself as a sociologist with an interest in psychiatry. But he did not publicly promote such a self-description over the long term; it would not have furthered his psychiatric practice and reputation. But it was accurate. And he was a polymath: sociology, anthropology, psychology, and the relationships among the three disciplines were his principal interest.

When he was directing his locked ward for schizophrenics at Sheppard Pratt Hospital, Sullivan considered it "a school for personality growth" rather than a psychiatric prison. [12] He focused on the non-medical dimensions of psychiatric disturbance, and on the non-medical treatment as well. He considered the interpersonal as the arena of health and sickness. Thus, he developed interpersonal treatments, with patients commingling by design with staff on a daily basis. He eschewed drug treatments, with at least one exception: he prescribed a limited amount of ethyl alcohol for certain patients over several days, allowing them to be mildly intoxicated in an effort to lower their social anxiety and build their interpersonal relationships. Because the Volstead Act, i.e., Prohibition, was still in force, outlawing the consumption of ethyl alcohol, he was severely criticized by some...even by his esteemed but puritanical former mentor, colleague, and son of a preacher, Adolf Meyer. [13]

❖ ❖ ❖

Sullivan was continually massaging Freudian concepts. He established his own zones of interaction, expanding Freud's original oral, anal, and phallic zones, changing phallic to genital, and inserting retinal, auditory, general tactile, and vestibular kinesthetic. He also contended that these zones were culturally variable, as in the case of American Indians who attended to auditory hallucinatory experiences. Furthermore, Sullivan regarded the oral zone as "the central trunk of the evolution of the self." [19]

Sullivan postulated that anxiety and security exist in polar relationship. He was attentive to patients, in all respects guarding carefully against furthering their anxiety. If for any reason he fueled their anxiety—as he sometimes deliberately did as a treatment tactic—he generally made sure that he had ample time to assuage it. Some of this urgency may have been derived from a former private patient, who left a session with him in a state of anxiety and immediately tied his belt around his neck in a suicide attempt. He did not die, but damaged his brain, and lived the remainder of his life in custodial care in a psychiatric hospital. That got Sullivan's attention. He contended that anxiety can never be deferred. Furthermore, sudden severe anxiety, Sullivan asserted, is probably never much more educative than a severe blow to the head.

The illusion of unique individuality, as Sullivan saw it, is a dangerous delusion. On the other hand, each person's pattern of interpersonal relationships is indeed unique, but it is only a relatively enduring pattern. No one should become too comfortable in what might be construed or presumed to be a unique and durable personality.

❖ ❖ ❖

There is only a thin blurry line that separates psychoanalysis and psychotherapy. The former connotes understanding and new awareness; the latter connotes healing. But both aim to do the same thing. An observer would likely have difficulty distinguishing one from the other in practice. And, very likely, a useful resource person does both tasks at once, analyzing and promoting healing.

❖ ❖ ❖

Neither the innovative Sandor Ferenczi nor the similarly innovative Sullivan thought that their modified methods were at variance with Freud's objectives. They felt that Freud was arguably too rigid on certain matters, such as the question of the personal boundaries and technique appropriate to psychoanalysis. As the founder of psychoanalysis, Freud was entitled to make that call, but he was deprived of the ability to make a final judgment on the matter. Even the not-very-flexible Otto Fenechel wrote, "everything is permissible, if only one knows why." Edith Weigert added that "fixation of rules is a danger for a science that has set liberation from compulsion as an essential goal." But Freud's concern was that both affection and hostility become tools of resistance, and must be analyzed, and not acted on. [14]

❖ ❖ ❖

Sullivan invested great energy in an effort to understand what psychotics were attempting to communicate in their anti-social behavior. He created a neologism in that effort, namely *audiation,* which he defined as *"hearing one's own voice."* [13] Sullivan worked at becoming more aware of his own verbal and non-verbal effect on patients in one way or another. He was continually attending to non-verbal communication in all its forms. One way in which he sometimes attempted to present a more human face was to have dainty finger food available on the arrival of a patient. Carlton Cornett cites one occasion in which Sullivan put a physically ill patient to bed in his home office. Otto Allen Will, Jr, the patient and later trainee, had arrived for an appointment very sick. (We do not know whether Sullivan would have done this for a female patient, but likely not.) Eventually, Will became a notable therapist in his own right, and was devoted to Sullivan. Later, their relationship became personal, and they developed peer friendship.

❖ ❖ ❖

Sullivan's colleague and friend, David Rioch, observed that scientists work in controlled labs, and that explorers work in the uncontrolled uncertainty of the real world. Sullivan, he added, worked in the latter, and did not think of himself as either a theoretician or a scientist.

❖ ❖ ❖

Sullivan had his detractors in the psychiatric community. The notable Otto Kernberg, though to some extent an ally, was critical of Sullivan for neglecting the intrapsychic, which some others have considered a flawed charge. But the most glaring antipathy for Sullivan among his near peers came from the younger—by 20 years—Heinz Kohut, the founder of "Self Psychology," and his colleague Edith Jacobson, an early so-called Ego Psychologist. They each diagnosed Sullivan—whom they seem never to have met, and certainly never examined—as too mentally ill to grasp Freud's theories. Kohut consequently declined even to mention Sullivan's name in print. It seems likely that they diagnosed him on the basis of his writing, or on here-say. And it seems likely that their diagnosis was posthumous, because an insanity diagnosis of a living person from a distance would surely be grounds for a lawsuit. More likely, the basis for their scurrilous charge was the fact that their theories were quite similar, or at least Kohut's were, and Sullivan got there first. [18]

❖ ❖ ❖

Erikson's *Childhood and Society* (1950) also appears greatly influenced by Sullivan. But he was rather stingy in referencing Sullivan, according to F. Barton Evans III. Evans also contended that Sullivan's theories are embedded today in British object relations theory. The short version of all this is that Sullivan seemed to have significantly shaped all post-Freudian psychiatry, but that virtually no one in the profession chose to acknowledge the fact. [18], Evans, *op. cit.,* pp. 4, 10, 81] Thus we see that Sullivan's work was ubiquitous in psychiatry in the time both before and after he died, but that his name was rarely mentioned. Evans suggests that Sullivan was essentially buried alive due to his extremely biting assessment of so many of his psychiatric colleagues. The profession of psychiatry was really a vicious clan—and may be still—but Sullivan's motto seemed to be: "damn the torpedoes."

We note with interest the very useful and professional anthology, *Inside Out and Outside In: Psychodynamic Clinical Theory and Psychopathology in Contemporary Multicultural Contexts,* edited by Joan Berzoff. This collection, contributed to by some dozen or so, mostly female psychotherapists, demonstrates the current reputational status of Sullivan. The 500-page volume features 19 essays and proposes to provide an overview of the field. Sullivan is named only twice (plus one duplicate), in a cursory manner, and by the principal editor herself. First, Berzoff cites Sullivan (Chapter 10, p. 222) simply as an early theorist. Then, along with Flanagan and Hertz (Chapter 13, p. 288), she quotes Sullivan: "We are all much more simply human than otherwise, be we happy and successful, contented and detached, miserable and mentally disordered or whatever." Lastly, in their "Conclusion: Some Final Thoughts," the authors repeat the same quote. If this is an important overview of current psychiatric thinking—and I believe that it probably is, and nicely done, generally speaking—then the contention that Sullivan's contribution to the field has been mostly deleted from psychiatric memory and history is demonstrated boldly in this collection. In the Berzoff anthology, Sullivan essentially is a nobody. [19]

However, one must not be too critical of Berzoff. She was simply reflecting the general ethos of the psychotherapeutic culture after Sullivan. He had indeed become a nobody. Sixteen years earlier, in 1995, the monumentally comprehensive review of all the psychotherapies and psychoanalyses by the inimitable and incomparable Robert S. Wallerstein, in a 587-page volume entitled *The Talking Cures: The Psychoanalyses and the Psychotherapies*, had established what was then the party line in psychiatry. And that book was what Otto Kernberg called "the most systematic study of the theory and practice of psychoanalytic psychotherapy that I know of...profound and original." But Wallerstein had continued the blackballing. He gave Sullivan the tag line of insignificant, with nine passing comments and two cursory footnotes, all of which add up to the implication that Sullivan was not really very important. He did allude to the possibility that "the gulf that had separated Kohut, Winnicott and Sullivan" may indeed have been exaggerated. And of course, he was correct. But Wallerstein did not pursue the matter, and he showed no evidence of having studied Sullivan himself. But who can blame him? Reading Sullivan in the original is a full-time job. The consequence was that Wallerstein continued the years of psychiatric blackballing 46 years after Sullivan's death. [20]

Wallerstein, like Berzoff, was simply following the oral tradition to the effect that Sullivan was not all that significant a player in the field of psychiatry. That tradition was established earlier in the highly regarded Harvard University Press's 1983 publication of *Object Relations in Psychoanalytic Theory,* by Jay R. Greenberg and Stephen A. Mitchell. [21] It purports to examine various schools of Object Relations. Sullivan's work is included as one among twelve schools of thought, although interestingly he is not named personally in the section headings, as everyone else was, as a key player.

The Greenberg-Mitchell explication of Sullivan's thinking is clear, accurate and insightful, a solid contribution to the field. However, no credence was given to the proposition that Sullivan may well have been central to serious and progressive psychoanalytic thinking in the world after Freud. Furthermore, Greenberg and Mitchell leave a couple of straws in the wind, suggesting a continuing unexamined discomfort with Sullivan, and perhaps even a covert wish on their part to make him disappear, or at least to remove him from any pedestal on which we might find him. The book's "Contents" page lists key players in the object relations field in its headings, specifically: Freud, Klein, Fairbairn, Winnicott, Guntrip, Hartman, Mahler, Jacobson, Kernberg, Kohut, and Sandler. Why not Sullivan? His approach to psychiatry is elucidated under the chapter entitled, not "Sullivan," but "Interpersonal Psychoanalysis." This seems a covert signal that Sullivan as a person, unlike all the others, is either especially significant or especially insignificant. Innuendo suggests the latter. Truth is that Sullivan was more of a *person* than any of the others named.

And in what used to be called "a Freudian slip," Greenberg and Mitchell described Sullivan as having "studied medicine during the 1920s in Chicago." That was decade later than Sullivan's actual time in medical school. Placing Sullivan a decade later in history makes it possible to minimize his influence. Sullivan was already publishing articles in psychiatric journals in the early

'20s, not attending medical school. Greenberg, Mitchell, Wallerstein, Berzoff, along with the bulk of psychiatry's leadership, were simply following the call of the American Psychoanalytic Association in 1949 in their attempt, as soon as Sullivan died, to erase him from history. They did a fairly good job of fulfilling that commission.

Contrariwise, one could make the argument that Sullivan was the root inspiration and source of all object relations theory and practice. One might argue that the singular source of this radical expansion of Freud's therapeutic—object relations—in all its manifestations was derived directly from Sullivan's interpersonal psychiatry. If we had to name one person who was arguably the prime source and inspiration of all object relations, self psychology, attachment theory, identity crisis, ego psychology and the like, it would be Harry Stack Sullivan. To put it another way, Sullivan was the first to expand Freud's focus on the unconscious with an additional focus— arguably a more important one—on interpersonal relations, and that all the other listed captions are little more than variations on the theme of Sullivan's *interpersonal*.

❖ ❖ ❖

Sullivan leveled a number of criticisms against Freud, but they must be weighed against Sullivan's entire corpus of comments on Freud. On balance, Sullivan was respectful and appreciative of Freud, even if at times he appeared in Sullivanian fashion to ridicule him severely, though playfully, as it seems to me. The reader must be careful about assuming that any one particular statement of Sullivan's was the last word. He was inconsistent, at points criticizing Freud, and at other points acknowledging his greatness. But on balance Sullivan acknowledged Freud's genius and his debt to him. In a similar way Sullivan confessed to having learned from Jung, but his ultimate assessment of Jung was on balance quite negative. The Jungian system, Sullivan contended, such as "its racial unconscious, according to which you are a sort of bud on a great reservoir of God knows quite what… with its racial unconscious is too preposterous to be taken seriously." Such systems, Sullivan said, "bore me too much by the nature of their speculation to be taken seriously." [22]

❖ ❖ ❖

In Freud's construct there are two drives, one propelled by sexuality and the other by aggression. Sullivan simply expanded and fine-tuned Freud's drive theory, in which was the body under stress reacts to seek and to recover a homeostatic state. Sullivan simply added love and the seeking of love. In fact, he placed that drive at the center of his theory. It is not far-fetched to assume that Freud, in retrospect, would have agreed. Life is far more than simply sex and power. And even Freud's practice was, as he himself put it, "a cure through love."

❖ ❖ ❖

Thus, Sullivan redefined psychiatry as the study of interpersonal relations. This was a bold and assertive claim, and by making it, Sullivan made himself, *ipso facto,* the principal voice of psychiatry in his generation. In so doing, Sullivan expanded Freud's drive theory by embracing and focusing on the interpersonal. He did not make Freud's construct irrelevant. He simply complemented it with the addition of interpersonal relationships, a subject which Freud seemed to minimize. Sullivan contended that what we do with each other as persons is critical to our psychological health and well-being; even our sanity. It seems that every psychologist since Sullivan has incorporated Sullivan's emendation of Freud, each apparently devising his or her own special language, making themselves appear original. [23]

The really dramatic declaration that Freud made, very late in life with only a decade more to live, was to clearly remove psychotherapy and psychoanalysis out from under the authority of the medical profession. This radical move further empowered Sullivan, who was already headed in that direction. It also empowered Anton Boisen, permitting him to identify himself as a psychotherapist. Freud laicized psychotherapy. The unfortunate part of it was that he was aging out, which permitted psychiatry to ignore him. And it only temporarily empowered Sullivan and Boisen, who by the time they died, were virtually erased from history. Nevertheless, Freud did pave the way, and early in the twenty-first century the iron grip of medicine on the work of psychotherapy was broken. A straw in the wind was the New York State licensing board permitting laypersons to become licensed psychoanalysts at the turn of the century, some seventy-five years after Freud called for it.

Freud published his opinion on the issue in 1926, just as Sullivan and Boisen were getting underway. He wrote that he never thought of himself as a "real doctor." He confessed that he had no occasion to use his medical knowledge in his psychoanalytic work. "A professional lay analyst will have no difficulty in winning as much respect as is due to a secular pastoral worker," he wrote. "Indeed, the words, 'secular pastoral worker' might well serve as a general formula for describing the function which the analyst, whether he is a professional or a layman, has to perform in his relation to the public." What the analysis can do for the patient, said Freud, is to

"...enrich him [the patient] from his own internal sources, by putting at the disposal of his ego those energies which, owing to repression, are being inaccessibly confined in his unconscious, as well as those which his ego is obliged to squander in the fruitless task of maintaining these repressions. Such activity as this is pastoral work in the best sense of the words." [24]

Sullivan also, whether following Freud or striking out on his own, made psychiatry and psychoanalysis into a non-science. As a participant observer the psychiatrist cannot be, by definition, a full-fledged objective observer. As a participant he cannot be a traditional clinician who is blind to the patient as person. Of course, Freud himself had also seemed even earlier to abandon science as the platform on which psychoanalysis could stand.

"Perhaps Harry Stack Sullivan's most important, fundamental, and neglected contribution was his extraordinary theory of personality, which may be more properly put as his vision of humankind," wrote F. Barton Evans III. [25] As Evans so astutely put it, Sullivan's vision of humankind was the foundation of his theory of personality. And founded on interpersonal relationships, I would add that Sullivan's personality theory has the stuff that could revitalize and make more relevant to humanity all the religions of the world.

The classic psychiatrists—Kraepelin, Freud, and Jung—oriented their insights to the individual and his or her *makeup*. Sullivan, on the other hand, focused on the individual in his or her *relationships*, the arena of the interpersonal and the social. Sullivan even went so far as to propose that individual identity is itself an illusion. That is a shocking proposition, but the more one attends to it, the more persuasive it becomes. [26]

---

1. Perry, Helen Swick. (1982). *Psychiatrist of America: The Life of Harry Stack Sullivan*. Cambridge: The Belknap Press of Harvard University Press.

2. Evans, F. Barton III. (2006). *Harry Stack Sullivan: Interpersonal Theory and Psychotherapy*. Oxfordshire: Routledge, Taylor & Francis Group.

3. Blitsten, Dorothy R. (1953). *The Social Theories of Harry Stack Sullivan*. New York: The William-Frederick Press.

4. Sullivan, Harry Stack. (1947). *Conceptions of Modern Psychiatry*. Washington, D.C.: The William Alanson White Foundation. This

monograph had a long and varied history. In its embryonic iteration it was the five-session address of the first William Alanson White Memorial lectures, in delivered in November 1939. In 1940, it was edited and appeared in the journal *Psychiatry*. Next, in 1945, it was printed in book form, but circulated only to students. On December 31, 1947, it was reprinted for the commercial market, a year and a few days prior to Sullivan's death. A final edition was published in 1953. It would be interesting to review each of these editions and to assess the changes that were made en route.

5. Sullivan, Harry Stack; Introduction by Helen Swick Perry. (1965). *Personal Psychopathology*. Washington, D.C.: The William Alanson White Foundation.

6. Perry, *op. cit.*, p. 199.

7. Sullivan, Harry Stack. (1953). *The Interpersonal Theory of Psychiatry*. New York: W. W. Norton & Company, pp. 3–30.

8. Evans, p. 82.

9. Rioch, David McKenzie. (1985). "Recollections of Harry Stack Sullivan and the Development of his Interpersonal Psychiatry." *Psychiatry,* 48:2, pp. 141–158.

10. Bettelheim, Bruno. (1984). *Freud and Man's Soul*. New York: Vintage Books, p. 42.

11. Sullivan, *CMP*, p. 142–143.

12. Sullivan, *SHP*, p. 264.

13. Perry, *op. cit.*, pp. 240–241.

14. *CMP*, 63–4, 137; *ITP*, 124, 282.

15. Blitsten, Dorothy R., *The Social Theories of Harry Stack Sullivan*, p. 61.

16. Wallerstein, Robert S. (1995). *The Talking Cures*. New Haven: Yale University Press, pp. 5, 23, 73.

17. Sullivan, *SHP*, p. 257.

18. Cornett, Carlton. (2017). *Being with Patients: An Introduction to the Psychotherapy of Harry Stack Sullivan, M.D., and Otto Allen Wilk, Jr., M.D.* (2018/paperback). Kingston Springs, TN: Westview, pp. xv, 2.

19. Evans, *op. cit.,* p. 10. [Kohut, Heinz. (1994). p. 411, declaring Sullivan mentally ill; also Jacobson. (1955). p. 150, cited by Carlton Cornett, *op. cit.,* p. 2.

20. Berzoff, Joan, ed., with Laura Melano Flanagan and Patricia Hertz. (2011, Third Edition). *Inside Out and Outside In: Psychodynamic Clinical Theory and Psychopathology in Contemporary Multicultural Contexts.* Lanham, MD: Rowman & Littlefield Publishers.

21. *CMP,* p. 39.

22. Otto F. Kernberg, on the back cover of Robert F. Wallerstein, *op. cit.*

23. Greenberg, Jay R. and Stephen A. Mitchell. (1983). *Object Relations in Psychoanalytic Theory.* New Haven: Harvard University Press, p. 81.

24. Sullivan, *The Fusion of Psychiatry and Social Science*, With Introduction and Commentaries by Helen Swick Perry, W.W. Norton & Company, New York, 1964, p. 258.

25. Sullivan, *TPI,* p. 3.

26. Freud, Sigmund; James Strachey, trans. and ed. (1926, 1927, 1969). *The Question of Lay Analysis.* New York: The Norton Library. Postscript to the 1926 SE, pp. 108ff.

27. Marco Conci makes the very interesting observation that Sullivan and Wilfred Bion are "imaginary twins" as pertains to the issues they dealt with, and the language they used. He says that each man oscillated between the relational and the drive model, and that each throws a very interesting and peculiar light upon each other." Conci, Marco. (2019). *Freud, Sullivan, Mitchell, Bion, and the Multiple Voices of International Psychoanalysis.* New York: IPBooks, pp. 3, 68.

CHAPTER 5

Sullivan and Boisen Converge

⚬⚭⚬

The precise date on which Boisen visited Sullivan at Sheppard Pratt, and met for the first time, is not recorded. It must have been sometime between the fall of 1924 and the spring of 1925. Subsequently, Boisen wrote, "I saw him many times after that, always with increasing respect and affection." [1] It seems that the feeling was mutual. Boisen was communicating with Sullivan even before he convened his first clinical pastoral training group in the summer of 1925, and continued to do so until Sullivan died in 1949.

Boisen and Sullivan had much in common. Each had experienced psychotic breaks. Sullivan, being a physician, was sensibly less candid about his own personal psychiatric suffering, but according to Perry, he did share with her and at least one other friend the fact that he had had a psychotic episode in 1908 when he was about 16 years old, was hospitalized, and that he was grateful that he dodged a lobotomy and electric shock. He expressed his fear that he might have become a permanent vegetable in the back wards of a hospital had the wrong physician gotten hold of him. Kate Frankenthal, a colleague of Sullivan's, disclosed to Perry in May 1970, that Sullivan had told her late in his life that he had had a severe schizophrenic episode early in life and "still had them." Obviously the episodes were not debilitating enough to require hospitalization. The testimony of Perry and Frankenthal seems substantive enough to conclude that Sullivan was, like Boisen, a chronic schizophrenic. But both men were obviously high-functioning types. [2]

There is a presumption that Sullivan was treated in 1908 or 1909 at Bellevue Hospital in New York City by Abraham Brill, the first of Freud's protégés to come to the U.S., who was on the staff at the time. Brill and Sullivan demonstrated later that they were personally close. Brill demonstrated in open discussions that he held Sullivan, 18 years younger than he, in great respect. At a seminar in 1929, Brill made pointed references to Sullivan's psychiatric knowledge. "Dr. Sullivan has the capacity, I might say schizoid capacity, to wax wittily and instructively about the nature and meaning of schizophrenia. Whatever he told us about the subject I can assure you that it is entirely true.... There are very few observers in this country who have devoted as much time to schizophrenics as Dr. Sullivan, so that his statements are authoritative.... I once differed with Sullivan, who contended that the progress of schizophrenics with olfactory hallucinations was invariably bad. Further investigation has taught me that Sullivan was correct." [3] (In a curious coincidence, Abraham Brill, the premier psychiatrist in the United States, served as a prime consultant to Theodore Dreiser while Dreiser was working on his Chenango County-based novel, *An American Tragedy.*)

❖ ❖ ❖

Both Boisen and Sullivan surmounted their own psychotic experiences to become central figures, in fact dominant game-changers in their respective professions. And oddly enough, each of them ultimately was subjected to posthumous historical amnesia in their own specific disciplines, and as well in the culture at large.

Sullivan at that time, in the middle 1920s, was on the cusp of having unusual success with schizophrenic patients, success that no one except his sometime mentor, Edward Kempf, thought possible. The patients in Sullivan's small experimental ward were all males, as was the entire staff. Furthermore, Sullivan determined to train his hand-picked staff of nurses and orderlies to become functioning psychotherapists in their own right. They would unlikely ever receive credentials by one organization or another, but Sullivan had little regard for such pro-forma certifications. He opened his home to his staff, seemingly at all hours. There he offered them impromptu training and consultation for their new role as "lay psychotherapist." He also provided refreshments—and meals.

On January 23, 1926, Boisen's article entitled "The Challenge to Our Seminaries" was published in *Christian Work: A Religious Weekly Review.* He too was in the process of transforming his own professional role. Boisen named four psychiatrists whom he recommended for his colleague, supporter, and later adversary Dr. Richard Cabot, to read. Boisen assumed that if Cabot had read these works, he would not be so sure that mental disorders were exclusively chemically or physiologically based—*and incurable.* Boisen was a bit naive in his assumption that a sometime-psychotic pastor could suggest a reading list for one of the alleged great physicians of the day, Richard Cabot, M.D., of Boston. And he did fail to succeed. In fact, this issue developed into the grounds for the ultimate termination of the close and creative Boisen-Cabot relationship in 1931.

The four psychiatrists Boisen named were Adolph Meyer (1866–1950), Charles Macfie Campbell (1876–1943), William Alanson White (1870–1937), and Thomas W. Salmon (1876–1927). In later years Sullivan himself would deserve a place at the top of that list. Both Meyer and White were mentors of Sullivan.

Meyer was a Swiss-born psychiatrist, ten years younger than Freud, who became the first psychiatrist-in-chief at Johns Hopkins and one of the most influential psychiatrists of the first half of the twentieth century. He generally but not unequivocally accepted Freud's claims for psychoanalysis and its declaration of the centrality of sexuality. As a Calvinist pastor's son, Meyer

77

also carried his father's conservatism, including an opposition to imbibing alcohol. Macfie Campbell became president of the American Psychiatric Association and joined Meyer at Johns Hopkins prior to ending his career at Boston Psychopathic Hospital. William Alanson White was Superintendent of St. Elizabeths Hospital and the preeminent American psychiatrist of his generation. He became Sullivan's therapist, mentor, consultant, and gadfly, whom Sullivan both loved and hated, but ultimately regarded as critical to his own development as well as the development of psychoanalysis in general. Thomas W. Salmon was Medical Director of the National Committee for Mental Hygiene. In Boisen's recommendation to Cabot of these four authorities, he demonstrated that he was familiar with the works of some of the leading figures in psychiatry of his generation; most unusual for a cleric. I doubt Boisen had any idea that the man he was now befriending would eventually eclipse the influence of each the four principals on his recommended reading list.

Boisen could not have referred any books by Sullivan because by 1926, Sullivan had not written any; it would be another two decades before a book by Sullivan appeared in public. He might have referred Cabot to Sullivan's journal articles, or even to Sullivan personally. But at that time, Sullivan was just coming into his own, a little fish in a little pond, and would not have much if any credibility in the eyes of the very-established Cabot at Harvard. Even Boisen did not yet know that Sullivan was in the process of radically upending the field of psychotherapy and psychoanalysis. In 1926, Sullivan was in midstream of his radical therapeutic work at the Sheppard and Enoch Pratt Hospital in Towson, Maryland, subsequently known simply as Sheppard Pratt. During the next quarter-century, Sullivan ultimately revolutionized psychiatry...simultaneously with Boisen's own revolutionary work in the training of clergy by way of the clinical pastoral training movement, a discipline Boisen actually created singlehandedly.

It is not certain how the Sullivan-Boisen relationship developed after their initial meeting at Sheppard Pratt. The next piece of data we have pertaining to their relationship is that of a letter written by Sullivan in 1927 to "My dear Mr. Boisen," confirming plans to meet Boisen at a luncheon. Attending data is not available. [4]

The first known reference to Boisen by Sullivan in print occurred in an article published in the *American Journal of Psychiatry,* [5] which was read before the American Psychiatric Association and the American Psychopathological Association meeting, New York, June 11, 1926, entitled "The Onset of Schizophrenia." (The article was reprinted posthumously in *Schizophrenia as a Human Process,* ed. Helen Swick Perry, 1962.) The citing of Boisen appears in a footnote: "See, for an interesting consideration not unharmonious with our views, Anton Boisen's 'Personality Changes and Upheavals Arising Out of the Sense of Personal Failure,' *American Journal of Psychiatry,* (1925–26) 82: pp. 531–552."

The two men were already cordially related enough by late 1928 for Boisen to invite Sullivan to join him in attending the Religion Section of the American Sociological Society Meeting in December, 1928, in Washington, D.C. At that meeting Boisen was scheduled to present the data from his first clinical pastoral training group at Worcester State Hospital for peer review. The fact that a lowly hospital chaplain invited the soon-to-become preeminent American psychoanalyst to join him for a sociological convention in Washington, in which he himself was presenting a case, is on the face of it astonishing. Boisen's paper was read aloud by a third party, a Dr. Hill from Worcester State Hospital. The University of Chicago professor of social ethics—and supporter of Boisen—Arthur Holt, presided. Animated discussion followed the reading. As Boisen reflected on the meeting later, he wrote of the discussion period: "I let it slip out that I believed that a conviction of sin was a first step in the process of salvation." Some in this gathered group of elite academicians responded negatively to this comment, perhaps mistakenly assuming Boisen to be some unsophisticated Christian fundamentalist. In Boisen's words, "All hell broke loose." As Boisen was getting pummeled by these academicians, Sullivan rose to defend Boisen's position in what Boisen described as "one of his characteristically keen and witty speeches...." [6] This suggests that the two men were already engaged in a significant relationship. A verbatim of Sullivan's rejoinder at that seminar would be worth more than its weight in gold, if it exists and could be found. Undoubtedly, Sullivan in his impromptu speech took no prisoners, as usual.

In August 1931, a letter from Sullivan to Boisen contained the salutation, "Dear Friend." Sullivan had visited Worcester State Hospital earlier that summer and sat in on Boisen's clinical pastoral training seminar. Sullivan reported in this letter that his visit to Worcester, where Boisen was Director of Chaplaincy, had been extraordinarily profitable, even though he felt that he had missed some of the things he had "wanted to discuss with Dr. Yorshis" and with Boisen himself. Then he commented that he hoped that his talk with Boisen's clinical pastoral trainees would gradually integrate itself into their experience to their profit. He expressed regret that he could not follow up with a clinical demonstration. He closed the letter: "With renewed assurances of my high regard, and the hope that we will be seeing each other again rather soon." [7] These bits and pieces confirm that Boisen and Sullivan were significantly related simultaneously with Boisen's creation of the clinical pastoral training movement.

Sullivan published an article in the *American Journal of Psychiatry*, 1931–32, (88:519–540) which had been presented at the 87th meeting of the American Psychiatric Association, in Toronto, June 5, 1931. Later, the paper carrying the title "The Modified Psychoanalytic Treatment of Schizophrenia" was incorporated as Chapter 11 in the collection of Sullivan papers entitled, *Schizophrenia As a Human Process, op.cit.* In the last two paragraphs of that paper, Sullivan seemed to meditate on the cultural effects on persons growing up in the quiet schizophrenogenic backwaters of rural America, which was surely autobiographical. He then stated that some ecclesiastics, who find joy in tinkering with the mild mental disorders in Church Healing Missions and the like, might learn much from the Rev. Anton Boisen, Chaplain at Worcester State Hospital. Boisen, who Sullivan averred, "has come by the tedious and often deeply disturbing road of observation and experimentation to a sane grasp of the relations of religious thoughts and techniques to the schizophrenic problem." [8]

Sullivan here is clearly taking a jab at Elwood Worcester and the Emmanuel Movement, a lay therapy movement centered in Boston early in the century and was still having some influence in its third decade. The movement was openly criticized by Freud and James Putnam as well. [9] Though Boisen himself was not as negative toward the Emmanuel Movement, he was clearly not uncritical of it. On May 21, 1952, two decades later, he commented on the matter in a letter to Otis Rice, President of Board of Governors, of the Council for Clinical Training: "The material from the Church of the Heavenly Rest recalls vividly the profitable days I spent with Dr. Worcester of Emmanuel Church in Boston. I do not recall any laying on of hands or any anointing with oil, but he did pray for particular persons and the spirit of the service was comforting and steadying...an atmosphere of hope and comfort... I am afraid I have not given you much help here. I am frankly not enthusiastic regarding healing projects of this type. And yet I do see possibilities here if the faith healing is combined with careful study of the individual concerned and the attempt to deal constructively with their problems." [10]

Then Sullivan closed his 1931 Toronto paper with a final short paragraph that seems to be autobiographical. "...if the young schizophrenic male... is received under care before he has progressed into either hebephrenic dilapidation or durable paranoid maladjustment, he will have a good outlook for recovery and improvement of personality... leading to socialization and... reorganization of personality." [11]

This same paper was incorporated later in the text of the First William Alanson White Memorial Lectures in 1939, which ultimately morphed into the only book Sullivan published in his lifetime, entitled *Conceptions of Modern Psychiatry*, and also incorporated into the four prior printings of the book by that name. But in the final posthumous edition of *Conceptions* in 1953, Sullivan has been dead five years, and Boisen is reduced to the following footnote: "This constructive effect of schizophrenic disorder, on which I published a paper in 1924, was at the same time under study by Rev. Anton T. Boisen, at the Worcester (Mass) State Hospital. For a statement of his matured judgments, see *The Exploration of the Inner World: A Study of Mental Disorder and Religious Experience*." [12]

Thus, within a half-dozen years of meeting each other, Sullivan and Boisen were respected public colleagues and personal friends, and Sullivan was citing Boisen with approbation in scholarly meetings and in published articles directed at social scientists. This is a clear commentary on the esteem in which Sullivan held Boisen, and vice versa, within their multi-disciplinary context.

❖ ❖ ❖

Boisen's "Problem of Values in the Light of Psychopathology" appeared in the *American Journal of Sociology* in July 1932. Several others of his papers appeared later in that journal. In 1933, Boisen wrote his "Experiential Aspects of Dementia Praecox," and the 33-page piece was published in the *American Journal of Psychiatry*. Other contributions appeared later. Still later, in 1958, he published in the *American Psychologist*. Boisen was conversant with current issues in sociology and anthropology as well as psychology and psychiatry. In his lifetime, Boisen's papers had appeared in four different psychiatric and sociological journals. [13]

The next surviving communication between Boisen and Sullivan is dated January 15, 1936. Boisen reported in a letter that he is now back at work…none the worse for his recent ordeal…and now facing the task of completing his manuscript for the publication of *The Exploration of the Inner World*. Boisen, as we know, had been briefly hospitalized himself at Sullivan's old hospital, Sheppard Pratt, in November of 1935. Boisen was showing psychotic symptoms simultaneously with the dying process of the love of his life, Alice Batchelder. He was hospitalized only four weeks, released after Batchelder died. The medical report on his release classified Boisen simply as "schizophrenic." His close friends had spirited him away from Chicago to Sheppard Pratt, where he was hospitalized until the symptoms dissipated. It was said that no one at Elgin suspected that he had been gone to be a patient in another psychiatric hospital. His friends kept the information private in order to help him maintain his self-respect. [14]

The next month, on February 11, 1936, Sullivan wrote: "Dear Friend, I would like very much to look over your material from your book." (*The Exploration of the Inner World)* Boisen had asked him if he would proofread some parts of it. [15]

On April 30, 1936, Sullivan wrote: "Dear Dr. Boisen, I shall read the chapter on my way to St. Louis. I shall not be able to visit you at Elgin, as I would very much like to do." [16] Boisen's move to Chicago four years earlier had put him physically close to Alice Batchelder as well as to the Chicago Theological Seminary, where he had been doing academic teaching part time since the middle 1920s. It also took him out of Cabot's now unfriendly orbit in the last few years of Cabot's life. (Cabot died in 1939.)

In the Foreword to *The Exploration of the Inner World*, published in 1936, Boisen stated that Dr. Henry J. Cadbury and Dr. Harry Stack Sullivan "have helped me with certain portions of the manuscript." He also thanked the *American Journal of Psychiatry* and the *American Journal of Sociology* for permission to use material of his, which they had already published. [17]

The next surviving letter was dated December 16, 1937: "Dear Mr. Boisen, It is always a pleasure to hear from you. I wish that I could plan to see you and your Council for Clinical Training Committee. I shall be in Chicago speaking to the local Psychoanalytic Society, and go to Topeka that evening." [18]

On January 4, 1938, Sullivan wrote under the letterhead of the William Alanson White Psychiatric Foundation, 158 East 64th Street, New York City, which he had just founded and now directed. He was announcing a new journal entitled *Psychiatry: Journal of the Biology and the Pathology of Interpersonal Relations*, printing 19,000 copies. Sullivan added: "I would esteem it a privilege if we could publish something from your pen…will you consider us as a mouthpiece?" Sullivan later dropped the journal's subtitle, which had been forced on him, and the journal became simply *Psychiatry*. [19]

On May 10, 1938, Boisen wrote to Sullivan: "I'm glad to hear that my paper has not been found unacceptable. [Boisen had submitted a paper to the new journal, *Psychiatry*.] Is the journal accepting books for review? I will be glad to send mine. Thus far this book of mine [*Explorations of the Inner World*] is pretty much a dud." [20]

❖ ❖ ❖

On November 13, 1939, Sullivan wrote:

Dear Friend:

I am very sorry to say that I have to deliver the fourth lecture in the series memorial to Dr. White, in the Interior Department auditorium in Washington the evening of the 17th. There seems to be no possibility of taking part in your conference in New York City, under the circumstances. I am there Tuesday and Wednesday only and this week and next, can make no change.

I am very sorry to have to pass it up and to have to disappoint you.

Cordially, [21]

On April 10, 1944, Sullivan wrote:

Dear Friend:

This is what might truly be said to be a delayed acknowledgement of your kind greetings in the holiday season. I have a schedule that expends my energy just about completely and put off everything which I would like to do well. This has included writing a decent letter.

I was delighted to learn that you have completed another book [Presumably *Religion in Crisis and Custom*, published in 1945] and wonder precisely what phases of our joint interest it is concerned with. I have accumulated a good many inches of transcript of a series of lectures which I hope to edit this summer and convert into the long overdue book.

As ever, [22]

On June 5, 1944, Sullivan wrote: "Dear Dr. Boisen, I believe I shall be reaching Chicago sometime the week of July 23, quite possibly Monday, the 24th...." Sullivan expected to spend a day and a half at Elgin State Hospital and Boisen's clinical pastoral training program there. Sullivan added: "I wish it might be possible for you to prepare a brief paper on your findings on this trip for publication in our journal [*Psychiatry*]." By "this trip," Sullivan was referring to Boisen's earlier visit to the camps for wartime conscientious objectors, a five-week review for which he was commissioned by the National Council of Churches. Boisen's report of that study was published in *Psychiatry* in 1944. [23]

On June 12, 1944, Sullivan wrote:

Dear Dr. Boisen:

It now appears that I must leave Chicago for the Southwest on Wednesday, July 28. Monday and Tuesday, July 24 and 25, seem to be the days I could have in Chicago.

Please do not feel in any sense constrained to make any awkwardness about schedule or the like as I would frankly be glad to have no more work until fall.

As ever, [24]

Sullivan was at that time having increasing health problems and was advised by his physicians to slow down. In less than five years, he would be dead from a cerebral hemorrhage.

On June 23, 1944, Boisen wrote to Sullivan providing a proposed schedule for his two days at Elgin. He also reported that Dr. Read had expressed his gratitude in advance to Sullivan for his impending visit, and that Dr. Read expected Sullivan to be his guest at his home on Monday night.

Sullivan arrived as scheduled that July 24 at the Chicago train station, on his way to New Mexico. Here's how Boisen described his arrival:

"As the time of his visit approached I wrote to him, asking him to let me know when he would arrive, and by what train. I received no reply and did not know what to do. Finally, on the morning of the appointed day, I received a telephone call. Dr. Sullivan was waiting in the Baltimore and Ohio Station in Chicago, 40 miles away. I hurried in and found him pacing nervously up and down, holding by the leash one of his favorite cocker spaniels, and with two heavy bags piled up on the side. I was certainly glad I had not suggested he take the interurban train! He gave two splendid lectures at our hospital and a superb demonstration of his technique of interviewing patients." [25]

Boisen wrote to Sullivan on June 19, 1945, a year later: "I have been drafted this summer to serve as consultant for all our Council's fifteen training centers." [26] It is not clear that Boisen was aware that Sullivan was seriously ill in the early months of 1945 and was seemingly at risk of dying. His local friends and his adopted son, Jimmie, spelled each other in caring for him.

On July 23, 1945, Sullivan wrote to Boisen:

Dear Friend,

I am very sorry that it was entirely impossible for me to see you while you were in Washington. Not only am I buried in work, but I am so low in energy that I simply can not do anything but rest in the evenings. I was too late to reach you at St. Elizabeths, and never found the telephone trunks to Gallinger free in the intervals in my next day's schedule.

I am knocking off work the end of this week until the middle of September, hoping to spend the last four weeks in Canada. The book should really materialize to a significant degree in those seven weeks.

I gave the first half of a course of thirty-four lectures this year, which seems to have realized my hope that they would be the conceptual skeleton for the presentation.

I hope it will not be too long before we have an opportunity for a visit.

Cordially yours, [27]

The book Sullivan is referencing is *Conceptions of Modern Psychiatry,* which was being readied for its 1947 publication—the first time it was to be available publicly and bookstore-ready. "Trunk lines" refer to the way intercity phone service worked in that era. One was not able simply to make an intercity phone call. Trunk lines had to be available, and in my personal memory, often were not, especially at times when they were needed.

On August 4, 1945, Boisen wrote to Sullivan:

Dear Dr. Sullivan:

I appreciate very much your note of July 23. I had learned while in Washington of your illness of some months ago, and I appreciated the fact that you did not have too much time or strength to spare. I am very much interested to learn that you are at work on that book again. It is much needed. I have wished many times that the lectures which appeared in Psychiatry could be published even as they stand.

I am leaving tomorrow for a return to the East, but my visit to Washington will probably occur before the end of the month.

Cordially yours, [28]

No record of that visit by Boisen to Washington seems to be available.

On December 5, 1946, Helen Swick Tepper (who later married Perry) wrote to Boisen to inform him that his article was accepted for publication in *Psychiatry*. Boisen wrote back expressing his appreciation on December 9.

On April 17, 1947, Boisen wrote Tepper to say that a patient who was discharged as "cured" has now been readmitted, and hopes this does not require a change in the paper that he is preparing for publication in *Psychiatry*.

Boisen visited Sullivan in Washington in early 1947, and wrote the following thank you note on April 9th:

Dear Dr. Sullivan:

It was a great pleasure to see you again on my recent trip to Washington and I appreciate your giving me so generously of your time. I was especially glad to learn that your *Conceptions of Modern Psychiatry* is to be made available for those who do not have access to the back numbers of *Psychiatry*.

My application for a grant-in-aid went in to the Public Health Service on March 22. Word comes from them that it is being prepared for consideration by the Advisory Council at their meeting on April 21–22. Apparently I was not too late. If there are any wires you can pull in my behalf, I shall of course appreciate it. Favorable action ought to mean a great deal to the undertaking of ours.

Faithfully yours, [29]

What Boisen means by "the undertaking of ours" must simply be speculated upon. The language reflects explicit collegiality between this psychiatrist and this pastor. It also connotes a matter of import. I presume that the undertaking is the training of ministers to be effective psychotherapists.

No evidence exists that the two men ever met again. In the summer of 1948, and again in the following winter, Sullivan was consulting much of the time for the United Nations in Eastern Europe, France, and Belgium, and died in Paris on January 14, 1949, two days prior to his scheduled flight home. There are likely to have been other letters and phone conversations between Boisen and Sullivan that are lost, or not otherwise accessible... potentially many of them.

Regarding the relationship between Boisen and Sullivan, we must conclude that they were very much allies and friends for a quarter century, and that their respective views on psychiatric disorders and approaches to healing were quite congruent. At some level, difficult to assess at this point, they may have been *dear* friends. Certainly the data show that they had very much in common, and surely there was a continuing high degree of cordiality and warmth between them.

The scholar Hendrika Vande Kemp goes so far as to assert that Boisen may have had as much influence on Sullivan as vice versa. I doubt there is data enough to confirm or deny that contention, but it is a credible thesis. [30] We can surmise that it must have meant a great deal to Sullivan that Boisen was a sometime *fellow psychotic,* and he must have admired Boisen's freedom to discuss such a personal and potentially damaging matter publicly.

Both Sullivan and Boisen were very much loners. Both men's sexual histories were most eccentric, and each was far outside the parameters of sexual practice of the average American male of any sexual orientation, likely in quite opposite directions. Neither man married.

I contend that Sullivan and Boisen were, in a real sense, soulmates. They each experienced psychotic episodes; Boisen's number of episodes seemed to have topped Sullivan's in both quantity and seriousness, though one cannot be sure. Boisen was quite candid about his psychotic breaks; Sullivan far less so about his own psychopathology, and only alluded to such experiences obliquely or privately to close friends. As a physician, of course, he certainly knew that he had too much to lose were he known to be a sometime psychotic; a realistic assumption. Each man struggled in one way or another with sexual identity. Some of the few surviving letters between the two men seem to be quite personal. Over the course of the last decade of Sullivan's life, he published in his *Psychiatry* journal nine articles and book reviews written by Boisen, who was certainly the only pastoral clinician in the twentieth century to have been published in such quantity in preeminent psychiatric and sociological journals.

That Anton Boisen, as a pastoral clinician and minister, developed such a significant personal and professional relationship with the man who was arguably the preeminent American psychiatrist of the twentieth century, is nothing short of astonishing. And that the historical memory of this alliance was essentially erased from public memory, both in the psychiatric world and the clinical pastoral world, is even more astonishing.

The riddle as to the nature of their friendship remains unsolved. It is not likely that they met to imbibe French brandy in the evenings. I doubt they addressed each other as Harry and Anton…but, maybe. The salutations in their letters, though friendly, are not on a first name basis. Boisen seems a little too stiff for that. Boisen's last known letter to Sullivan in the spring of 1947 following their meeting in Bethesda communicates a deep respect and admiration. Boisen expressed his appreciation to Sullivan for giving his time. I suspect that Sullivan was Boisen's crypto-therapist, who also happened to be his friend. But perhaps Vande Kemp is correct—that Boisen was also Sullivan's therapist in a certain way. I surmise that they were colleagues in the same field who liked and respected each other, and that Boisen probably learned more from Sullivan than vice versa. I further believe that Sullivan aided Boisen in keeping at bay his proclivity for psychotic episodes. But it may in fact have been vice versa, or both-and.

So how was it that both Sullivan and Boisen were the objects of corporate amnesia in both the subsequent clinical pastoral movement and the discipline of psychiatry? In one sense, the question is bereft of an answer. In another, it is easy to guess why. History shows us that rejection and/or amnesia is a common response to very creative and innovative persons who challenge too many basic assumptions in a given time and social order.

Boisen, who lived to age 89, experienced an especially long and personally degrading decline. Sullivan died suddenly at a relatively young age, a few weeks short of his 58th birthday, but immediately became a virtual non-person in the field of psychiatry. Boisen lived on another 16 years. His name continued to be edified even beyond his death in 1965, but it became a name without substantive content. His written work was almost entirely ignored by those who populated the movement he founded, and his books went out of print. The clinical pastoral movement trudged on, bereft of Boisen's central teaching, that religious leaders must play a psychotherapeutic role. In a reverse way, in psychiatry, Sullivan's name was mostly erased, whereas his innovations were adopted and reformulated as if others had newly discovered them. The attention to interpersonal relationship in the work of psychiatry, as an expansion of the Freudian focus on the unconscious, became almost universal in international psychiatry, but with no credit among his American colleagues given to Sullivan, who assuredly deserved much, if not all the credit.

The mystery as to what drew Sullivan and Boisen together seems to persist. I suggest that it was their mutual experiences with episodic psychoses. For Boisen, after his treatment by psychiatrists during his first incarceration, at Westboro, the psychiatrists' sermonizing, telling him that he must change his thinking about sexuality, left Boisen with a feeling of contempt toward them. He wanted them to listen to him, not provide advice on changing his behavior. This contempt was reinforced from Boisen's reading, while hospitalized, Freud's *Introductory Lectures*, the book that changed his life. And subsequently, in Sullivan, Boisen found a psychiatrist who actually listened to him, understood him, and at the same time valued him as a friend and colleague. After Sullivan died, Boisen expressed remorse, indirectly. There was no one to replace him. The specialness of Sullivan for Boisen was that he did not attempt to block or negate his psychotic episodes, but simply related to him as a friend. He may have provided some level of therapy as well, but that is not in the record. The details of their relationship remained obscure.

With the death of Sullivan, Boisen seemed to feel that he had lost psychiatry in general. In his Foreword to the 1952 Edition of *The Exploration of the Inner World*, he wrote: "So far as concerns that body of organized and tested experience which is known as 'psychiatry,' it has in large measure fallen by the wayside. My hope for this reprinting is that it may help to recall attention to it." [31] It was Sullivan, of course, who in death fell by the wayside, and there was no one with his wisdom and his love to replace him in Boisen's world.

Why, then, did Sullivan appreciate Boisen as a "friend," as he often addressed him? Boisen was likely both a friend and a quasi-patient. Boisen depended on him, and undoubtedly Sullivan helped Boisen maintain an even keel for a quarter century. Thus, Boisen became what Sullivan was not permitted to be, a competent successful public professional while simultaneously being an episodic psychotic. Boisen's earlier eight-year bonding with Richard Cabot, M.D., went on the rocks after Boisen experienced his second and brief psychotic episode in 1930. Cabot then radically altered his earlier assessment of Boisen as a change agent for clergy. Suddenly, Boisen, in Cabot's eyes, was no longer even qualified for ministry, much less to be a trainer of ministers. Cabot then moved to oust him from the very Council for Clinical Training that Boisen himself had created. But the attempt backfired: Cabot instead was ousted, mainly by the assertiveness of Boisen's principal supporter, the psychiatrist Helen Flanders Dunbar. The promising relationship between Richard Cabot, M.D., and the Reverend Anton Boisen was ended. One can only imagine what Cabot would have said about Sullivan. (Perhaps he did indeed somewhere comment on Sullivan, since Cabot lived until 1939.)

So, what did Sullivan find so appealing in Boisen that he went to such lengths to support him publicly and in writing and to build a personal relationship with him? I propose that Sullivan saw in Boisen what he wished to see in psychiatry but could only dream of: that a psychiatrist would not be required to hide his own psychotic episodes in order to function professionally. Sullivan of necessity lived a double life and was constantly and of necessity engaged in deception; a requirement not placed on Boisen. This was undoubtedly a painful burden for a man as sensitive as Sullivan. It was also a severe distraction, undoubtedly limiting his creativity.

The Committee that sponsored the five collections of Sullivan's writings consisted of six psychiatrists who loved him and sought to make sure that his voice was not lost to history. However, by Helen Swick Perry's account, the Committee decided that it should not register any suggestion that Sullivan himself may have had a psychotic episode or multiple episodes. Even in death Sullivan had to disguise himself and pretend he was not what he was.

Was their decision contaminated by shame over the possibility that Sullivan was an episodic schizophrenic? When Helen Swick Perry proposed as much in her role as Editor in her introductions to the volumes, the Committee objected. Astonishingly, they opposed printing any suggestion that Sullivan may have been hospitalized for psychiatric treatment, thus playing into the hands of Kohut, who categorically dismissed Sullivan on the grounds that he was "insane." Episodically speaking, Kohut was surely correct. His guiding principle seems to have been that an experience of psychosis disqualifies one from becoming a psychiatrist. Given this stance, one can thereby understand why Sullivan so appreciated Boisen. Here was an admitted episodic psychotic who was eminently successful in bringing the vocation of pastoral ministry into the modern world by transforming pastors into "pastoral psychotherapists," adepts of Freud!

I suggest that the question of whether or not to own up to the evidence that Sullivan had had psychotic experiences created division within the

Publication Committee of Sullivan's Writings, and not simply in relation to Perry vs. the Committee itself. I note that in the list of Committee members who worked on the last three of the five collections, the two women who, after Perry, probably loved Sullivan the most—Janet MacKenzie Rioch and Clara Thompson—were no longer participants. Sullivan was Rioch's analyst, while Thompson was his longest and arguably closest woman friend.

A generation after Boisen's death, a new group, the College of Pastoral Supervision and Psychotherapy (CPSP), organized in 1990 and began certifying pastoral psychotherapists. It was a small act of reclamation of Boisen's principal thesis: that clinically trained religious professionals are indeed psychotherapists. But this organization, too, had no memory of Sullivan. His name had vanished from the conversation of pastoral clinicians in every context.

On the other hand, the older, more established branch of Boisen's clinical pastoral movement, the Association for Clinical Pastoral Education (ACPE), focused increasingly on *education* rather than *psychotherapy*. Their practitioners are referred to as *educators,* not therapists. What the future holds for either community is not yet clear and will reveal itself in due course.

---

1.   Boisen, Anton T. (1960). *Out of The Depths: An Autobiographical Study of Mental Disorder and Religious Experience.* New York: Harper & Brothers, Publishers, p. 156. (Hereafter, OOD.)

2.   Perry, Helen Swick. (1983). *Psychiatrist of America: The Life of Harry Stack Sullivan.* Cambridge, MA: The Belknap Press of Harvard University, pp. 34, 154, 337, 444.

3.   Perry, *op. cit.*, p. 154.

4.   Chicago Theological Seminary Library, archival letter file for Anton Boisen, hereafter "CTSL".

5. Sullivan, Harry Stack. (1927–28). "The Onset of Schizophrenia." American Journal of Psychiatry, 84: pp. 105–134.

6. Boisen, OTD, p. 166.

7. CTSL.

8. Note: Sullivan's article, "The Onset of Schizophrenia," published in the *American Journal of Psychiatry*, and appeared in the 1927-28 issue (84:105-134), was also read in abstract before the joint meeting of the American Psychopathological Association in New York, June 11, 1926. Sullivan wrote in a footnote, "See, for an interesting consideration not unharmonious with our views, Anton Boisen's "Personality Changes and Upheavals Arising Out of a Sense of Personal Failure" [*American Journal Psychiatry* (1925-26) 82:531-552). It seems quite remarkable that Sullivan, who had met Boisen face-to-face in the fall of 1924 at the earliest, was now touting him publicly as a psychoanalytically informed pastor. There is no known account of their first meeting, but it must have been significant. Also included in SHP, p. 272, is an address entitled "The Modified Psychoanalytic Treatment of Schizophrenia", delivered to the eighty-seventh meeting of the America Psychoanalytic Association on June 5, 1931, and reprinted in SHP, p. 272. The next to the final paragraph refers to Boisen as the chaplain at Worcester State. "There are some ecclesiastics who find joy in tinkering with the mild mental disorders, in church healing missions and the like. These folks might learn much from, for example, the Rev. Anton Boisen, Chaplain Anton Boisen, Chaplain of Worcester State Hospital, who has come by the tedious and often deeply disturbing road of observation and experimentation to a sane grasp of the relations of religious thoughts and techniques to their schizophrenic problem. That was clearly added later when Sullivan's paper was incorporated into his first book, distributed in *Psychiatry* in 1940. The cited Boisen book, *Out of the*

Depths, was not published until 1936. By then, Boisen had left Worcester and was at Elgin in Chicago.

9. See Stokes, Allison. (1985). *Ministry After Freud.* New York: The Pilgrim Press, p. 5, *passim.*

10. CTSL.

11. Sullivan, Harry Stack. (1962). *Schizophrenia as a Human Process.* New York: W. W. Norton & Company Inc., p. 290.

12. Sullivan, Harry Stack. (1953). *Conceptions of Modern Psychiatry.* Each of the seven times Conceptions was published, the wording of the footnote citing Boisen was subject to slight modifications. The first public edition was dated December 31, 1947, with Sullivan adding a Foreword and Dexter M. Bullard adding a Preface. It also features a Clinical Appraisal of the Theory by Patrick Mullahy. Previous editions were published for students and colleagues, and not circulated in the wider public. Each printing or edition featured some editing

13. CTSL.

14. OTD, p. 177.

15. CTSL.

16. Boisen, Anton T. *The Exploration of the Inner World: A Study of Mental Disorder and Religious Experience.* Chicago and New York: Willett, Clark & Company, 1936. (Hereafter, TEIW.)

17. CTSL.

18. CTSL.

19. CTSL.

20. CTSL.

21. CTSL.

22. CTSL.

23. CTSL.

24. CTSL.

25. OTD, p. 184; Vande Kemp, Hendrika. "Harry Stack Sullivan (1892–1949): Hero, Ghost, and Muse." In *The Psychotherapy Patient* (2004), Vol. 13, p. 42. Philadelphia: The Haworth Press, Inc.
26. CTSL.
27. CTSL.
28. CTSL.
29. CTSL.
30. Vande Kemp, Hendrika, *op. cit.*, p. 1.
31. TEIW. Forward to the 1952 Edition.

CHAPTER 6

The Later Sullivan

ᐧᐤᐧ

S ubsequent to the end of the war on November 11, 1918, Sullivan bounced around in a variety of medical jobs that never quite satisfied him. Sullivan's first real job as a psychiatrist was his appointment by the United States Veterans Bureau in November 1921. He had been appointed a "neuropsychiatrist" in the position of Liaison Officer to the federal mental hospital in Washington, D.C., St. Elizabeths. He was required to be approved by the Superintendent, the powerful Dr. William Alanson White, which he was. But when he asked White about the possibility of full-time clinical work, his answer was that there were no posts available. However, in less than two years a position opened up for director of a new, experimental ward at Sheppard and Enoch Pratt Hospital, in Towson, Maryland, commonly referred to simply as Sheppard Pratt, a humanistically oriented psychiatric hospital founded by Quakers in 1853. It was the first psychiatric hospital established in the U.S. [1]

Sullivan went to Sheppard Pratt in 1923 as a novice psychiatrist, and he left under pressure in 1930 as a legend in the world of clinical psychiatry and psychoanalysis. Being a legend did not help him keep his position; quite the contrary. Even those who appeared to appreciate Sullivan for most of a decade—like his mentor William Alanson White—supported his removal from Sheppard Pratt. (Although, it must be said that White supported him in certain other ways.)

No specific reason for Sullivan's dismissal from Sheppard Pratt was made public. Perhaps it was due to the galaxy of Sullivan's idiosyncrasies. Rumors of homosexuality undoubtedly loomed large, but *sotto voce*, especially in that more homophobic—and sex-phobic—era. Moving a troubled, vagrant 14-year-old boy into his home certainly must have added fuel to that fire. Treating his patients with small amounts of ethyl alcohol for a period of several days—to create a mild state of intoxication in order to loosen up their social interactions—caused political blowback from law-abiding teetotalers, even though such treatment was found to be beneficial for psychotics, just as it can be for normal neurotics at a cocktail party. Sullivan was correct therapeutically, but this was still the era of Prohibition! Though the Volstead Act was soon to be blessedly overturned, a significant part of the population still supported it. Even the esteemed psychiatrist and Sullivan's former mentor and *teetotaling* colleague, Adolph Meyer, was offended by Sullivan's violation of the Volstead Act. [2] On the other hand, physicians are permitted to prescribe a wide range of drugs. Why not alcohol? Rumors also spread that Sullivan borrowed and failed to repay money from friends, but confirming rumors is a difficult, obnoxious, and often fruitless assignment. None of his friends seemed to be complaining about his burdening them. He did declare bankruptcy in 1931, but so did many others during that economic Depression. And then, there were Sullivan's acerbic, iconoclastic public comments that were unnerving to so many. But probably what worked against him more than anything were his boundary-testing comments and proverbial sayings pertaining to sex. The Hollywood-drenched but paradoxically sexually repressed culture of the American middle class at mid-century did not make a happy home for Sullivan.

Sullivan published a summary farewell statement addressed to his colleagues at Sheppard Pratt. He called them to their task: "Let us, as psychiatrists and particularly as teachers of medical students...renew our efforts to preserve 'the man as a person' from total extinction within medicine...the teaching of an elementary knowledge of how men live, love, hate and deceive themselves—[and then]...your graduates will be prepared for the seventy percent of their patients' troubles with which they now have no ability to cope." [3]

Sullivan was a voice in the psychiatric wilderness. He also inveighed against lobotomies, which the American Psychiatric Association finally condemned almost two decades later in 1948. As Perry put it, Sullivan was too much of a gadfly for too many politically powerful persons in the American Psychiatric Association, the Rockefeller Philanthropies, and at the National Committee for Mental Health. They simply wanted to be rid of him.

Upon being terminated from Sheppard Pratt in 1930, or more accurately resigning under pressure, Sullivan moved to New York City and set up a private practice. He certainly did not roll over and play dead. One of the first things he did was to pay a visit to his friend, Anton Boisen, who was Chaplain and Director of the Clinical Pastoral Training Program at Worcester State Hospital in Massachusetts. There he met with Boisen's Clinical Pastoral Training group and also with the medical and administrative staff.

Seeing the writing on the wall, Sullivan had already moved his office to New York City in 1929 and set himself up for private practice in anticipation of his departure from Sheppard Pratt. He soon fell into financial difficulties, living in the high rent district of the upper East Side of Manhattan. He is said to have borrowed money from several friends, including $3,050 from Clara Thompson. But he continued imbibing 100-year-old French brandy. There is no record of his having had an alcohol problem, however...nor is there any evidence that Thompson ever complained about an unpaid debt.

Sullivan was hardly a penny-pincher. He was generous even when in debt. He opened his Manhattan home to a wide variety of friends who needed a place to live. His guests, who came and went, included such varied characters as Erich Fromm; Philip Sapir, the son of his friend and anthropologist colleague, Edward Sapir; Patrick Mullahy, a young Irishman who was eventually to write a commentary on Sullivan; and Katherine Dunham, the black dancer who was a former patient of Sullivan's. According to A. H. Chapman, Sullivan claimed to be the best-paid psychiatrist in New York City, which Chapman says may well have been true. If so, that money slipped rapidly through his fingers. He freely loaned money to needy friends, but he in turn continued to borrow money, including $2,000 from Abraham Brill. The summary picture of Sullivan as pertains to money is that he had no regard for it, either to possess it, or to owe it. [4]

Another one of his quirks, reported by A. H. Chapman, is that he rarely looked his friends in the eye, attributed to his years of working with schizophrenics who were uncomfortable with anything resembling a stare. For such patients, he made only the slightest eye-to-eye contact. [4]

In the context of his private office, in contrast to the Sheppard Pratt ward, Sullivan generally refused to treat schizophrenic patients, according to David Rioch. [5] Office visits for schizophrenics would not provide the kind of communal 24-hour therapeutic community that he believed they needed, and that he provided at Sheppard Pratt. And of course, there was sparse hope of being paid for treating the typical walk-in schizophrenic. While Sullivan had a history treating indigents without charge, he was now housed in a high-rent district, and on the ropes financially. Building a significant income was not an optional objective. What's worse, he had moved there in the midst of the infamous Great Depression. As he wrote to his friend Lola White, "The development of private practice in the depression of the century is no little stress and tribulation." [6]

❖ ❖ ❖

Sullivan had harbored hopes of moving into psychiatric education on his departure from Sheppard Pratt. But he needed financial backing. There were financial resources available in various endowment agencies, but politics rolled over Sullivan, and he failed to receive backing from the American Psychiatric Association for this work. White, ever with his eye on the political landscape, also declined to back him. Sullivan had by 1930 become a psychiatric gadfly in too many contexts, but more especially within his own discipline of psychiatry. Sullivan wrote to White, "The axe has descended on my hope for an immediate beginning of progress on the psychiatric education matter." [7] White predictably reminded Sullivan, *again*, that "[He] had failed to observe the amenities, and thereby frustrated himself." But Sullivan was not wrong. Psychiatry was, and still is as a discipline, all over the map.

In his new life, Sullivan, relatively free from institutional inhibitions, asserted himself. He nominated himself as chair of the new "Joint Commission on Psychiatric Education." He sought to spearhead a psychiatric Flexner Report, which was greatly needed, but he was never able to garner quite enough support to make it happen (and it still has not happened). It is probable that Sullivan imagined himself as the psychiatric Flexner, and in such a role, he might have humanized psychiatry in a dramatic fashion. On the other hand, a psychiatric Flexner Report done by someone like the original Flexner may well have put Sullivan out of business as a dangerous outlier.

Sullivan's failure to get enough support to spearhead an examination of current psychiatric practice was, according to Perry, a "pointed rebuff—-one from which he never recovered." And the legendary White was the main force behind the rejection. However, Sullivan and White did continue to maintain a cordial social relationship, such as birthday greetings and expressions of concern about sickness, and such. He also had a very warm relationship with White's wife. And Sullivan continued to trumpet White's name, even after White died in 1936. [8]

A year later, Sullivan resigned from the American Psychiatric Association's Committee on Psychiatric Education, saying, "...the axe has descended on my hope for an immediate beginning of progress on the psychiatric education matter." Then he wrote an article, which was published in the *American Journal of Orthopsychiatry* in 1931:

> "Let us by all means gird our loins—if any—for the salvage of the mentally ill...let us by some sublime means focus in the stillness of our studies—or bath rooms—on the present state of psychiatry... casting aside our compensations, sublimations and defense reactions, retrieving our repressed and dissociated materials, and reversing our regressive tendencies—let us bend our energies toward the assembling and refining of a sound body of information that will be the fundamental material for training all students. Voices crying in the wilderness are all right, but I could not find a dozen people, that I would unhesitatingly recommend as professors and heads of departments in psychiatry. I know a great many psychiatrists who know a great deal more about various aspect of psychiatry than I do. Many of them have discouraged me as to their suitability for the recommendation by presenting to me, personally, facts that I know are not facts. In other words, they know too much or too well—they are propagating errors, superstitions, or religion." [9]

The prophet Amos could not have said it better.

Sullivan addressed the American Psychiatric Association meeting in Toronto on June 5, 1931, the same lecture in which he paid homage to Boisen. He spoke on a method of treatment (his own) for schizophrenics, which was "rather intimately related to the psychoanalytic method of Sigmund

Freud," but suggesting a variation of Freud's technique. He went on to speak of the "future of each physical-chemical organism…. which may exist in some reality underlying our hypothetical time-dimension." The future of each person "must be recognized as a function of the eternally changing configuration of the cultural-social present." [10]

Sullivan then made a strange and befuddling prediction about his own life:

"Conceivably, it was in some ultimately comprehensible fashion ordained at the moment of the writer's conception that he shall cease to live owing to rupture of the middle meningeal artery at the age of 57 years, three months and five days, plus or minus less than 100 hours." [Sullivan, *SHP*, p. 274]

Sullivan died on January 14, 1949, aged 56 years, 10 months, and 24 days, notes Helen Swick Perry in a footnote. He overestimated his longevity by five months but accurately foresaw his cause of death. His autopsy in Paris was performed by Dr. Charles Paul, the Police surgeon, who determined that the death was undoubtedly natural, caused by "a rupture in the meningeal artery with lesions in the liver and kidney." I have never come across any attempt to explicate this stunning prognostication. What can be made of this is anyone's guess. It is surreal. [11]

Prior to leaving Baltimore, Sullivan instituted a regular Monday dinner with his two closest Baltimore friends and fellow psychiatrists, Clara Thompson and Billy Silverberg. Meeting in Thompson's home, they socialized and discussed cases. In the cases that they discussed, they discovered that those particular patients seemed ultimately to do better than most. So they began calling their Monday gatherings "The Miracle Club." When Sullivan later more fully moved to New York City, as had Clara Thompson, he replicated the club, but expanded it to include others, meeting in a speakeasy, and renaming it "The Zodiac Club." Each participant was required to select an animal in the zodiac to represent themselves. Sullivan chose the horse, as he was since childhood, "the son of the west wind riding east to meet the dawn." Thompson was a puma, Silverberg a gazelle, and Jimmie, his adopted waif who sometimes joined them, a seahorse. Karen Horney, who joined them later, was a water buffalo. Eric Fromm was a member, but seems to have abstained from playing the zodiac game. Horney ultimately turned on Fromm for his lack of an M.D. degree, resulting in his dismissal from the American Psychoanalytic Society, and ultimately, to his moving to Mexico City in 1949. Later, Karen Horney herself was dismissed from the American Psychoanalytic Society for being abusive to students. Psychiatrists are worse than Christians, repeatedly shaming each other. So much for professional collegiality.

Thompson reported that the group became more and more organized into Sullivan's thinking. The members of the Zodiac Club eventually and unaccountably morphed into being referred to (not of their own choosing) as "Neo-Freudians," a moniker without substance. [12] Anyone relating to Freud is either Freudian or anti-Freud.

During 1930, Sullivan filled in for the editor of the *American Journal of Psychiatry*, Edward N. Brush, who had fallen ill. During that year Sullivan instituted a national census on psychiatric education in his continuing effort to clarify what psychiatrists were actually learning, a sort of embryonic Flexner Report for psychiatry. Brush commended him for that. A year later, Brush resigned and recommended Clarence G. Farrar for the position of editor. Sullivan, though the most prominent person on the staff, was not considered. Brush's valedictory address at his final banquet made no mention of Sullivan's leadership or contributions in the transition. Again, the contempt in which the moguls of psychiatry held Sullivan, and the way they treated each other, was astonishing. [13]

Sullivan got back on his feet through connections with the polymath Harold D. Lasswell, benefactor Ernest E. Hadley, and the Yale anthropologist Edward Sapir. In one of his many visits with Sapir, beginning in the summer of 1932 at Sapir's summer home in New Hampshire, he encountered the anthropologist Hortense Powdermaker, who was spending the summer with Sapir after her year-long work among the Lesu people in Papua New Guinea. She was preparing for her upcoming work "with blacks in Mississippi." Sapir was one of the principal scholars who touted Sullivan's importance as well as the importance of integrating psychology and anthropology, a vision dear to Sullivan himself. Sullivan was to have many subsequent visits with Sapir in New Haven, where he was teaching. They formed a significant bond. On occasion, Sullivan joined Sapir in the Yale classroom.

When the summer was over, Powdermaker traveled to Fisk College in Nashville to meet with Charles S. Johnson, chairman of social sciences, and Franklin E. Frazier, Professor of Sociology, to determine the best ways to approach her proposed fieldwork in Mississippi. Seven years later, Sullivan followed her path, making his own trip to the same part of the state and similarly conferring with Fisk. It was from that visit that Sullivan wrote that "the no-man's land of the pantry in a white Southern upper-class household was one of the few places in Mississippi where a white man could appropriately observe a black man." Knowing Sullivan, he was certainly relating as well as observing. A decade later, Johnson was to give a eulogy at Sullivan's funeral. [14]

In 1936, Sullivan, still in New York, co-founded the William Alanson White Psychoanalytic Institute. White, who late in life became less than enthusiastic about Freud, forced a change from *Psychoanalytic* to *Psychiatric*. After White died, Sullivan became the institute's *macher* (big shot), whether one liked him or not. "Psychoanalytic" was reinserted into the White Institute name. In returning to the Washington area, Sullivan also founded the Washington School of Psychiatry, but it did not emerge as a significant institution until 1943. Today, each of these institutions claims Sullivan as their founder. However, the William Alanson White Institute website seems to highlight Clara Thompson and Erich Fromm over Sullivan, even though it does recognize Sullivan as its founder.

During the last decade of Sullivan's life, from 1938 to 1948, the tide of fortune turned in his favor. His detractors did not vanish, but his accomplishments overshadowed them. William Alanson White, his mentor and sometime supporter—and thorn in his side as well—died in March of 1938, giving Sullivan more space. But the New York psychoanalysts became increasingly obstreperous. Sullivan moved back south, to Bethesda, Maryland, in the Washington area.

That same year, Sullivan co-founded the journal *Psychiatry* with Earnest E. Hadley, and after several years—subsequent to a gentlemanly dispute and a friendly settlement—took it over entirely. Sullivan remained Editor-in-Chief, and ruled it for the remaining ten years of his life.

As it turned out, the William Alanson White Institute, along with the Washington School of Psychiatry and the journal *Psychiatry*—along with his teaching platform at Chestnut Lodge—were to become Sullivan's potent pulpits of continuing influence for the short remainder of his life. With the death of White, Sullivan had lost an ambivalent supporter while simultaneously being liberated. Except for Chestnut Lodge, the three other Sullivanian institutions continue to function today.

Moving back to the Washington area, to Bethesda, Sullivan was euphoric when, later the same year, he was unexpectedly appointed as professor and chair of the newly created Department of Psychiatry at Georgetown University Medical School, a relatively liberal Catholic school. The Board of Trustees approved him on October 14, 1939. He went to work immediately and enthusiastically, designing his new program. Within several days, someone in authority spied the words *psychoanalysis* and *Freud* in his curricula. That information was passed on to the Board with haste, which reconvened and ousted Sullivan before he even received his first paycheck. The Catholic authorities who owned the University wanted no part of Freud, psychoanalysis, or anything related, but the Church had no objection to giving him a big funeral a decade later, with Catholic and military honors, at Arlington National cemetery. Certainly, they were glad to see Sullivan's ashes laid in the grave. [15]

In any case, Sullivan was almost certain to have gotten himself into trouble with the Catholic leadership at the University eventually, a liberal Catholic university though it was said to be. Though nominally a Catholic himself, Sullivan wrote in a lecture given in 1942 that "the Society of Friends was the most astonishing demonstration of there being a Christian way of life that I've ever encountered—in fact, almost the only one." He did not leave much of any opening for the Catholic Church. The founders of Sheppard Pratt were Quakers, which likely had much to do with his view. [16]

Quite an interesting exchange took place just prior to Sullivan's dance with Georgetown. The previous year, Sullivan had sent a copy of Boisen's *The Exploration of the Inner World* to Dom Thomas Verner Moore in Wisconsin for a review to be published in *Psychiatry*. No review was forthcoming in the expected timeframe. In March 1939, Sullivan's secretary sent a query to Moore asking when the review would be completed. No reply to that query is recorded. But the query was approximately simultaneous with Moore's appointment to the Catholic University in Washington as head of the departments of Psychology and Psychiatry. Sullivan likely was unaware of these developments. It has to be doubted that Moore, in his constrained Catholic context, would have gone public—unless negatively—on a monograph like Boisen's, which lauded Freud in the way it did. [17]

A month later, Sullivan hit the ground running, presenting the first William Alanson White Memorial Lectures, a series that he himself had devised after White's death. He delivered the first series himself, consisting of five lectures, which ultimately, after a decade of editing, morphed into the book, *Conceptions of Modern Psychiatry*. Subsequent White Memorial lecturers were the likes of Henry Wallace, Abe Fortas, and Martin Buber.

On December 5, 1940, Sullivan was asked to become the psychiatric consultant for the Selective Service Board under Director Clarence A. Dykstra. It was an unpaid position, but the Carnegie Foundation provided a grant for support of the work. Sullivan traveled to major cities to lecture and give seminars to Selective Service Boards. Sometimes he paid for his own transportation because of the tight budget. Roosevelt replaced Dykstra as Director in 1942 by a military man, Lewis B. Hershey. Hershey considered himself to be an amateur psychiatrist, and consequently terminated Sullivan sometime in 1942. At a post-war party, Dexter M. Bullard, Director of Chestnut Lodge, asked Hershey what the problem was between himself and Sullivan. "No problem," replied Hershey. "We both wanted to run the Selective Service, and there was room for only one of us." (As an editorial aside, it has to be suspected that Hershey was blowing smoke. More likely, he was privy to gossip about Sullivan and decided to be rid of him.)

In October of that year, Sullivan became a regular lecturer at Chestnut Lodge in Rockville, Maryland, arguably the premier psychotherapeutic treatment center in the country at the time. For the rest of his life, as his health and schedule permitted, he met twice a week as lecturer and consultant with the Lodge's therapeutic staff and visitors. Dexter Bullard recognized Sullivan's gifts and gave him freedom of the city, so to speak. Both he and (especially) Frieda Fromm-Reichmann sat at the feet of Sullivan's genius. Sullivan ultimately gave 246 lectures at the Lodge to a variety of listeners. They were recorded, presumably on wire recorders, and apparently are still accessible. The recordings ultimately became and remain a significant reservoir of Sullivan's ideas. The lectures were said to be difficult to follow but certainly no more difficult than Sullivan's published works.

Sullivan's exacerbating heart disability threatened to reduce his activities to a low ebb. In 1945, he was under medical pressure to retire from strenuous activity. He was immobilized for a number of weeks with a serious illness that appeared to threaten his life and had to be closely cared for by Jimmie and several friends. Instead of retiring, Sullivan went to work for UNESCO. He attended conferences in Czechoslovakia in the summer of 1948, joining the noted anthropologist, Ruth Benedict, whose family home was, like Sullivan's, in Chenango County. Benedict died that September 17, at age 61, soon after she arrived home from Europe. Sullivan wrote a memorial account of her life. On September 24, his old friend and former chief at Sheppard Pratt, Ross McClure Chapman died. [18]

An analysand of Sullivan's, Janet MacKenzie Rioch, a pediatrician who had become close to Clara Thompson, also joined the Chestnut Lodge staff. Her younger brother David McKenzie Rioch, a research neurophysiologist who had a distinguished career at Harvard, Johns Hopkins, and Washington University in St. Louis, then joined the staff of Chestnut Lodge for the specific purpose of working with Sullivan, as did his wife, and my late friend, Margaret Rioch, a key figure in the later Tavistock movement, and who was an important player in the lay psychotherapy movement. [19]

Chestnut Lodge became the hub of Sullivan's influence for the remaining six years of his life. He helped make the Lodge's reputation as arguably the most progressive psychiatric treatment center in the nation. Frieda Fromm-Reichmann, a pre-war immigrant from Germany and protégée of Sullivan's, became the senior clinician at the Lodge, which became one of few psychiatric hospitals that focused on cures for schizophrenia. (Joanne Greenberg, also a friend of mine, and author of *I Never Promised You a Rose Garden,* was an inpatient there in her teens for a couple of years in the late 1940s and worked directly with Fromm-Reichmann, the fictional "Dr. Freed.")

Several different monographs discuss portions of the recordings of Sullivan's Chestnut Lodge Lectures, making use of only a fraction of them. [20] For the first time since he left Sheppard Pratt, Sullivan, according to

Perry, was in charge of his own life, and prospering. He was also in rapidly declining health.

After the war in Europe, Sullivan resumed his extended friendship with Major General G. Brock Chisholm, who ran the medical service for Canada in World War II, and who was the only psychiatrist ever to become Deputy Minister of National Health for Canada. Chisholm became the first head of the World Health Organization. Sullivan invited Chisholm to give the second White Memorial Lecture, in the fall of 1945. The two men shared a similar philosophy of psychiatry and psychiatric treatment. Each held the view that mental health was shaped not only by intrapsychic forces but also by the creative and destructive forces in society. [21] When Chisholm visited, the two men spent several days socializing, joined by several equally iconoclastic friends in Washington prior to Sullivan's William Alanson White lectures, and later also in New York City. [22]

(*Chisholm recounted a humorous story from his early* life. At about age six, he and friends were out for a ramble after Sunday school while their parents were in church. The children engaged in a discussion and concluded by assenting to the following thesis: "You have to believe in Santa Claus until you're six, but you have to be twenty-one before you may stop believing in Jesus." Sullivan is reported to have found that proposition exceedingly humorous and memorable.)

In the fall of 1945, Sullivan was advised by his medical consultants to slow down. After his serious heart problem the previous winter, he was advised that his life was at risk. But he decided that in light of the entrance into the nuclear age, he was called to work full speed ahead and do what he could. In Perry's words, he chose martyrdom, driving himself, and everyone else whom he could, to work for world order and world peace. "It appears that I'm about to make even more of a fool of myself than usual, but, by God, I'm going to do it!" He continued to drive himself hard for another three-and-a-half years. (White and Ferenczi had each set an example for him, working with those psychiatrically war damaged from European war of 1894–1895.) [23]

The William Alanson White Foundation held a Christmas party in December of 1948, and Sullivan attended, full of good cheer, but frail. He was dreading the rigors of yet another trip to Europe, this time to attend a meeting of the World Federation for Mental Health. He made it, but did not make it home. He died in his room at the Hotel Ritz in Paris just after being served breakfast, which was left untouched, on January 14, just two days before his scheduled flight home, and on his mother's birthday. There were rumors of suicide, but no supporting data. Perry, who knew Sullivan well, conjectured that given his frail condition, and the anniversary of his mother's death, he may well have lost the will to live, and might have misused his medications either accidentally or on purpose. Beyond such unsubstantiated conjectures, there is no evidence that Sullivan committed suicide, or even wanted to do so. [24]

Sullivan had specified his request for a Catholic funeral and burial at Arlington National Cemetery, with the full military folderol. He was a veteran of World War I, and worked for the Selective Service in World War II. Though not a churchgoer, he is said to have appreciated the austerity and beauty of the Catholic rites. But the Catholic part of the burial was a close call; he had been cremated in France, and the Church prohibited the liturgical burial of cremains. Ultimately, someone leaned on the Church authorities, and the Catholic funeral proceeded, his coffin containing only his ashes.

Sullivan's friends were flummoxed by his choice of Catholic burial rites. They never saw him anywhere near a Catholic Church nor heard him endorsing any form of Catholicism. My thought is that this request, aside from being driven by the artistic dimension of the funeral rites, was simply payback from the time he buried his mother, one of the very few Catholics in Chenango County with Catholic rites as she wished. The local Ku Klux

Klan burned a cross on a nearby hill within sight of the Sullivan home, presumably to celebrate her death. Sullivan surely never forgot this act of bigotry. We can assume, I believe, that the Catholic and military pageantry together was at least in part Sullivan's retort to the hostile pageantry of the Ku Klux Klan at his mother's funeral.

Sullivan's adopted son, Jimmie, sent a memo to Sullivan's friends and colleagues justifying the Catholic funeral. He quoted Sullivan: "Of all the church services, I prefer the Catholic because that service is the most unemotional, most impersonal, and beautiful." He also noted that Sullivan used to attend Christmas mass in New York City at the urging of and in the company of Dr. Libman, who was Jewish. He, too, appreciated the austerity and quiet emotion of the liturgy. [25] Whatever Sullivan's message, he was not even close to being a practicing Catholic.

The burial at Arlington was held four weeks after his death and was followed by a memorial service at Walter Reed Hospital's Sternberg Auditorium. Five members of the National Symphony Orchestra played Mozart's Clarinet Quintet, two movements from his Serenade in G, and the Adagio from Brahms' Clarinet Quintet. In later discussions with some of the mourners, "The Girl with the Flaxen Hair" was associated with Sullivan, but exactly how is not registered by Perry. Alfred H. Stanton, a younger colleague and student, spoke at the service. The sociologist and good friend of Sullivan's, Charles S. Johnson, then President of the African-American Fisk University in Nashville, also spoke: "It is tragically fitting that he should have reached the end of his life and work in Europe where the last bright fires of his zeal and skill have been devoted to the analysis of these tensions between nations and groups that lead men to war and to futile killings, that are leading the nations of the world into a new and perhaps last remaining great effort at mutual self-destruction." [26]

Then, Clara Thompson gave the Eulogy for Harry Stack Sullivan, the Man: "We have met here tonight to honor the memory of a man who has left a sense of loss in all our lives.... Harry Stack Sullivan was a lonely person from his earliest childhood.... He was the only surviving child of a poor Irish farmer in upstate New York.... All the other children died in infancy.... The mother, who thought she had married beneath her, was a complaining semi-invalid with chronic resentment at the humble family situation. She gave the young boy little warmth. In fact, he said she was not interested.... Although this farm boy had a long journey to go, something in him would not rest.... It was a few years later, when he first went to Sheppard Pratt Hospital...that our friendship began.... I soon learned that this man who in public could tear a bad paper to bits with his scathing sarcasm, had another side—a gentle, warm, friendly one. This was the side he showed his patients. Anyone who has seen him talking with a disturbed catatonic can know that he has seen the real Harry without pretense or defenses. There was nothing maudlin about his tenderness—it rather conveyed a feeling of deep understanding.... He was slow in making friends. He tested them for a long time.... Once a person had passed the test he could count on Harry for absolute loyalty.... In looking out for his own personal affairs Harry was strangely impractical. His head was in the clouds and his feet were often not on the earth. Perhaps this was to be expected from a descendent of the West Wind. For a hard-headed scientist this man had much poetry in his nature.... He was brought up as a Catholic and although his thinking took him far from formal religious beliefs, he retained a great fondness for the beauty and dignity of the Catholic ritual. He was deeply religious in the sense of believing in the positive qualities of man. He had a characteristic phrase when parting from a friend—"Gods keep you." This phrase always seemed to me to roll back a curtain and one got a glimpse of the Irish lad with the tradition of pagan gods. One could have no doubt that he meant, "May the good forces in your world protect you.".... His belief that a way could be found to bring lasting peace to the world was a fire within him which sustained his frail body in the last physically ill years of his life.... He will go on living with us and through us who have known him. He died the death of a hero in the midst of carrying on work dearest to his heart. Truly we have known a man of great stature." [27]

Sullivan had written his own epitaph:

"Begin; and let it be said of you,
if there is any more history,
that you labored nobly in the measure of man
in the XX century of the scientific Western world." [28]

---

1. Rioch, David McKenzie. "Recollections of Harry Stack Sullivan and of the Development of His Interpersonal Psychiatry." *Psychiatry*, 48:2, 1985, p. 143; and Perry, Helen Swick. *Psychiatrist of America: The Life of Harry Stack Sullivan*. Cambridge: The Belknap Press of Harvard University Press, 1982, pp. 176, 180.

2. Perry, *op. cit.*, p. 240.

3. Perry, *op. cit.*, p. 290.

4. Perry, *op. cit.*, pp.320-323.

5. Chapman, A. H. *Harry Stack Sullivan, His Life and His Work*. New York: G. P. Putnam & Sons, 1976, pp. 57–59.

6. Rioch, David McKenzie. *"Recollections of Harry Stack Sullivan and of the Development of His Interpersonal Psychiatry."* Psychiatry, 1985, 48:2, pp. 141–158;

7. Perry, *op. cit.*, p. 302.

8. Perry, *op. cit.*, pp. 289ff.

9. Perry, op. cit., p. 300.

10. Sullivan, SHP, p. 272.

11. Perry, *op. cit.*, p. 417.

12. Perry, *op. cit.*, p. 300.

13. Perry, *op. cit.*, pp. 357–8.

14. Perry, *op. cit.*, p. 385.

15. Perry, *op. cit.*, p. 362.

16. Chicago Theological Seminary Library, archival letter file for Anton Boisen.

17. Perry, *op. cit.,* p. 403.

18. Joanne Greenberg, personal communication.

19. Rioch, pp. 155–6.

20. See for example, Robert G. Kvarnes, ed. *A Harry Stack Sullivan Case Seminar: Treatment of a Young Male Schizophrenic.* New York: W. W. Norton & Co., 1976.

21. Perry, *op. cit.*, pp. 404–5.

22. Perry, *op. cit.*, pp. 416–20.

23. Perry, *op. cit.*, p. 421.

24. Perry, *op. cit.*, p. 423.

25. Excerpted from *Harry Stack Sullivan the Man*, by Clara Thompson, pp. xxxii–xxxv, in *Schizophrenia as a Human Process*, Harry Stack Sullivan, With Introduction and Commentaries by Helen Swick Perry, W. W. Norton and Company, New York, 1962. (First published in *Psychiatry* (1949) 12: pp. 435–437.)

26. Perry, *op. cit.*, p. 424.

CHAPTER 7

Boisen's Finale

∽∞∾

Sullivan was radically liberated sexually—in word at least, if not in deed, and likely both. Boisen, on the other hand, was so repressed and sexually inhibited that one has to wonder how the two managed to be such significant colleagues and friends for a quarter-century The matter remains something of a mystery. There is an absolute dearth of data on what either of them thought of the sexual posture of the other, although they clearly appreciated each other, and it is obvious from peripheral data that they held each other in high esteem. There is sparse record of the content of significant conversation between them on any particular issue, sex or otherwise; this, in spite of the fact that there were many meetings and phone conversations between them over a quarter of a century. Each was an astute clinician. But how did they negotiate the fact that Sullivan talked like an antinomian, freewheeling sexual liberationist, and acted as if he might be an active homosexual, or perhaps bisexual… and Boisen, like one who is sexually repressed, and massively so? With both men dead, and no known evidence that speaks directly to the question, it is unlikely that we will ever know the answer. A very good guess is that both men were extremely tolerant of the thoughts and feelings of the other and simply overlooked the apparent and presumed sexual quirks in the other. That is the way we all treat friends who are dear to us. Furthermore, I believe that their shared episodic schizophrenia along with their mission and commitment to promote healing of other fellow schizophrenics—and others—likely bound them to a common humanity, leading each to be tolerant of whatever flaws they observed in the other.

We know precisely about the root, as well as the progress, of Boisen's psychotic breaks, but we have very little, if any, authenticated data about Sullivan's. In Boisen's case, it was his full introjection of his mother's negativity about sex. He never recovered from it. In maturity he zeroed in on one unattainable love object, Alice Batchelder, who was the dream woman for a man like Boisen: the kind of woman whom Boisen's mother might have prayed for her son to find, with a massively repressed libido. While Boisen courted Alice indomitably for more than three decades, they almost certainly never engaged in more intimate physical contact than Boisen kissing Alice's hand. And even if Alice *had* offered Boisen a real kiss, or any erotically tainted act, he might well have restrained himself on the grounds that they were not yet married, or at least engaged. Alice was a kind of reverse image of Jephthah's daughter who, condemned to die a virgin at a very young age, mourned her virginity. [1] Anyone who delights in and affirms sexual pleasure would consider Alice to have been a shrew. But Boisen would not have spent much time with any woman who was not phobic about sex. (He seems to have had a brief flirtation with the liberated Helen Flanders Dunbar in the 1920s, but it is very unlikely that anything came of it.)

In relation to Alice, Boisen clearly diminished himself. It could be said that he placed Alice in the position that his mother held for him psychodynamically. Alice withheld from him any sexual access over a 33-year courtship, and strange as it may seem, Boisen honored her for that. She played her anti-libidinal role to perfection. As Boisen put it, Alice, being a woman of integrity and courage, was one to whom "I must first prove my manhood and the devotion I professed. This I failed to do." It must be recognized, he wrote, that "I was a really sick person who came to her for help. This help she at first refused, but eventually granted...my love for her has been a source of healing." [2]

Healing? Well, not quite. Though he accomplished great things, Boisen was never healed of his fear of lust. And Alice was a perfect helpmeet in assisting him in sustaining his fear of lust that his mother implanted in him at age four, and throughout his childhood. Boisen seemed unclear as to whether he pursued Alice for a satisfying personal relationship or for psychotherapy. Ultimately he claimed he got the latter, but actually he got neither. Boisen was certainly astute enough to know that Alice was no therapist at any level, but perhaps he needed to feel that she was, since she fulfilled his mother's ideal.

Some may wonder how Boisen managed with hospitalized mental patients, since a majority of their problems were indeed sexual. However, it is clearly shown in his case reports that Boisen was far more gracious to others in relation to their sexual desires, struggles, and indiscretions than he was toward himself. In fact, if that were not the case, he could hardly have worked as a pastoral psychotherapist in psychiatric institutions for as long as he did. He reflected a non-judgmental posture in relation to patients in his case studies, a graciousness he could never allow for himself.

As Boisen aged, however—and he lived to be 89—evidence suggests that he became increasingly difficult in his personal relationships, if not those with his patients. His later pastoral colleagues at Elgin State Hospital reported that he was disagreeable to work with as he got older. Herman Eichorn, who left his supervisory job with Boisen at Elgin in 1951, one year after taking the position, found Boisen impossible to work with. [3] Clarence Bruninga replaced Eichorn in 1955 and seems to have remained in the position until at least 1960. In a phone conversation with Bruninga on March 9, 2000, Bruninga told me that Boisen in his old age "did a good job of offending everyone who worked with him. It was a struggle working with him."

From the middle 1940s onward, Boisen seemed to become even more vexed over issues of sexuality, particularly the escalating post-war sexual liberalism. His own aging—he turned 70 in 1946—was likely a factor. Time was passing him by in this respect. In his *Out of The Depths,* published in 1960 but likely written for the most part earlier, Boisen launched an attack on English and Pearson's *Common Neuroses of Children and Adults,* a text widely used by clinical supervisors in their training groups. The book goes into fine detail about the Freudian construct of developmental stages of children as they face issues in the oral, anal, and genital developmental periods. (I found the book quite useful in my own training in the 1960s.) But the book troubled Boisen even though he continued to laud Freud. In reaction, he accused some pastoral clinicians of explaining George Fox (the Quaker founder) in terms of toilet training. He charged clinicians with swallowing Freudian theory without scrutinizing it. He accused pastoral clinicians of lowering the conscience threshold in order to accommodate erotic desires. He asserted that clinicians were abandoning the insights of the Hebrew-Christian religion for the sake of sexual freedom. And interestingly, he inveighed against Wilhelm Reich more strongly in his *Out of The Depths* than he did in his review of Reich's work published in Sullivan's *Psychiatry* journal. Of course, *Psychiatry* was directed at a different audience. Boisen was harsher with his fellow pastoral clinicians than he was with Reichians, as indeed he had a right to be, even if he was becoming a crotchety old man. [4]

And we must presume that it was no small matter for Boisen that Sullivan died in January of 1949. Sullivan was without doubt the major personal and therapeutic support for him for a quarter century, and there is no evidence of other significant support coming from elsewhere. Yet there is no mention of the loss of Sullivan in *Out of The Depths,* which is curious. The last mention of him in the book was pedestrian: "The outstanding feature of our programs in the summer of 1944 was a visit from Dr. Harry Stack Sullivan. While in Washington on the conscientious objection study, I learned that he was going to New Mexico in July, and I prevailed upon him to stop over at Elgin." [5] What he might have written was that his summer clinical pastoral training program was beneficiary of a two-day visit from the preeminent American psychiatrist of the twentieth century.

Sullivan's early death must certainly have been a great loss for Boisen, who lived another 16 years. However, no record of any significant mention of Sullivan posthumously or of his untimely death has yet been found in the archives. That constitutes a curious silence about someone who was a major support for 25 years. There is no evidence of a rupture between them subsequent to their last quite congenial face-to-face meeting in Washington in 1947, and for which Boisen expressed his appreciation in writing. [6] Following that visit, Sullivan lived less than two more years, much of which time he spent working for the United Nations in Europe.

Another loss for Boisen was the withdrawal of support, moral and financial, from the community he founded. When in 1946 he appealed to Fred Kuether, then Administrator for the Council for Clinical Training (CCT), for $3,000 to support a research project, the request was denied. The CCT in fact owed Boisen more than $3,000. Boisen claimed that he had no choice but to live in an Elgin Hospital storage room adjoining the refectory for lack of financial resources. The very organization that he had founded declined to assist him. Of course, there may be more to the story than is known. Suffice it to say, Boisen approached the end of his life in poor straits.

❖ ❖ ❖

Boisen's second book, published in 1945, was *Religion in Crisis and Culture: A Sociological and Psychological Study*. [7] It is a random collection of essays on a variety subjects, from slavery to the work of Christ to the Holy Rollers, and more. Indications suggest that the book was thrown together, a kind of *potpourri*. Under the section labeled "Crises in Personality Development,"

Part IV, section 4, is a chapter entitled "Acute Schizophrenic Reactions." In that chapter, Boisen presents two extended cases of schizophrenic patients with whom he himself had worked, giving them the names "Rudolph" and "Oscar." Both cases illustrate intense sexual conflict, but that is nature of the problem for the majority of hospitalized schizophrenics.

The Case of Rudolph

Rudolph, age 43, was hospitalized after a suicide attempt. Rudolph described his father as strict and his mother as kindhearted and "awfully soft." He grew up in a respectable middle-class family in Germany, and he emigrated to the U.S. at age 16. Earlier, at age 12, he had begun struggling with masturbation, with "unspeakable worry." He could not bring himself into harmony with the standards that he had intellectually accepted, says Boisen, who certainly must have identified with his patient.

Finally, as a young man, he was drawn to an evangelistic revival, where the hymns and preaching spoke to him. He stayed up all night praying and weeping and ultimately responded to the preaching of the revivalist, a Mr. Moody, and to the evangelical hymns. The results were that everything changed for him. For years subsequently, he was happy and successful in his work. He married a faithful member of the church, a woman before whom he stood in awe, as, in Boisen's words, he desperately tried to maintain or perhaps reconstruct his self-respect. For some years he remained stable, active in the church and continuing to be "awed" by his wife.

At some point, about 25 years later, Rudolph decompensated, and was finally hospitalized after an attempted suicide. Apparently, this is the point at which Boisen began working with him. "The realm of sex was still for him something at once fascinating and terrifying," wrote Boisen. He had desires and tendencies which he could not control and about which he was afraid to speak. "He had acute mental indigestion," wrote Boisen, whatever that may have meant. "The true evil in this case," wrote Boisen, "was the short-circuiting of the sex drive and the consequent failure to attain to the next level of development." On the meaning of short-circuiting of the sex drive, Boisen is obscure, but likely he meant a return to masturbating. By Boisen's account, Rudolph invested a great deal of personal energy in attempts to refrain from masturbating. Boisen gave it all away when he described Rudolph as one who "had wandered far from the admonitions of his pious mother." My conclusion is that Boisen himself, as one who resolutely had *never* wandered far from the admonitions of *his* pious mother, was not able to connect therapeutically with Rudolph in his suffering. He was likely much too identified with him negatively, an instance of projective identification.

Boisen ranted on: "The therapist must be quick to see through the shams and self-deceptions which are sheltering forbidden desires and are thereby blocking growth." The unsocialized and therefore unassimilated interests must be resolved, and "the sufferer must be able to feel himself restored to the *fellowship of the best*." Moody gave the right suggestions, according to Boisen. Now forgiven, Rudolph had something to live for. After subsequent backsliding, he later became institutionalized in a psychiatric hospital, and the implication is that he never recovered. "We must heal the breach between the ideal self and the actual self not by lessening the conflict but by heightening it," wrote Boisen. [8]

Boisen, as a reputable clinician in general, is notably obscure as pertains to exactly what was likely driving Rudolph's decompensation. Clearly, it was related to Rudolph's sexuality, but in exactly what way is not stated. It seems certain that Boisen envisioned sexual abstinence as Rudolph's prospective cure, that the abstinence had failed, and that otherwise, Boisen simply did not want to know.

Boisen's summation seems to have been that Rudolph, though in awe of his wife, was also fascinated and terrified by sex, or in Sullivan's more precise

125

language, his lust, and was not able to control and satisfy his sexual desires. Boisen implied that Rudolph was a hopeless case; apparently, Rudolph spent his last years in psychiatric incarceration.

In my view of this case, Boisen identified strongly with this patient and treated him with kindness and respect, but he nevertheless remained uncomfortable with Rudolph's persistent lust. Seemingly professional enough to avoid acting out with Rudolph, Boisen remained a victim of his own unresolved conflict about sexual pleasure; his countertransference got the best of him. Because he never recovered from his own fear and loathing of sexual pleasure, embedded in his psyche by his mother from age four, he had a crippling blind spot regarding matters of sexuality. Therefore, by extension, Boisen was not able to assist Rudolph or others who struggled with the same issue. Technically, in being too closely identified with Rudolph and not realizing it, Boisen failed in this case. He appears to have communicated to the patient that he, along with Evangelist Moody, supported Rudolph's sexual repression, the very thing that was oppressing him. However, we must keep in mind that Boisen did seem to listen to the patient and without condemnatory judgment. Listening itself, with a certain identification, is also therapeutic. Therapy itself is mostly listening. Sometimes patients recover in spite of the therapist.

The Case of Oscar

The second case in *Religion in Crisis and Culture* is that of Oscar, a stocky, muscular man of 53, also a European immigrant. He had had a previous psychiatric episode 13 years earlier. Boisen met him in the hospital when Oscar had just emerged from a second episode. As a youngster, Oscar hated school. On the other hand, he could lick any classmate. He went to sea at age 20 and eventually emigrated to the U.S. Oscar claimed to have had the usual struggles with masturbation in adolescence, but the difficulties were, in his words, "not excessive." He consorted with some prostitutes during his life as a seaman. At age 31, he married. His wife then became supreme in his system of loyalties.

Like Rudolph, Oscar idealized his wife. He claimed that his marital adjustment had been happy, and his wife agreed. However, his home life was something of a matriarchy. His wife reported, "He always says anything I say is alright." The impression is that the patient did not often assert himself. He confessed that he "never did grab anything in religion." His first symptoms were increased self-absorption, loss of sleep, pacing the floor, and moaning. He told his wife to go away, and she did. With that, he made a suicide attempt. He was found alive with the gas turned on and both wrists cut, "one for each of his daughters."

Thirteen years earlier at a Socialist meeting turned religious, Oscar had given his life to Christ, identifying with Jesus. He was delirious for three days, but recovered and went back to work. His wife was told at the hospital that Oscar's trouble came from reading the Bible, so he agreed to put the Bible in the attic. In the subsequent episode, he was told by the *voices* to go and retrieve the Bible. A voice asked him, "Are you willing to commit suicide?" He acknowledged that he did think of himself as Christ.

Boisen concluded that Oscar's psychosis was a desperate attempt at reorganization, which was to some extent successful. "He was unusually free from the malignant attitudes of suspicion, hostility, and *eroticism*," wrote Boisen (emphasis mine). Finally, God said to Oscar in a vision: "You was going right the way you was. (sic) I don't need you to preach. I have other men I can send." [9]

Boisen labeled such mental disturbances as problem solving. When the voices asked Oscar if he was willing to give up his life for others, the true answer to the question was that he already had; his psychosis was exposing an accomplished fact. Oscar had given up his life to his wife. She was now supreme in the household and in his system of loyalties. Even Boisen identified, and admitted, that it would be sometimes a bit trying to submit to her domination. On the other hand, Oscar was a carbon copy of Boisen himself, who in effect gave his life to both his mother and Alice Batchelder, each a textbook dominatrix…except in Boisen's case, he did not even get any companionship, housekeeping, and access to sexual pleasure in exchange.

Boisen contended that both sex-love and religion are attempts to achieve the same thing: union with the idealized other-than-self. He further stated, "…*sex love seeks something beyond the finite object of affection, and that it cannot be satisfied with the finite.*" (Emphasis mine.) Boisen goes off the rails here, projecting his own conflictedness over physical sexual pleasure; or as he labels it, pejoratively, *eroticism.* We must conclude that, brilliant and psychotherapeutic as he was in so many respects, Boisen was not very competent in his attempts to provide psychotherapy for persons suffering from conflict over lust. But Boisen did listen, and seemingly without judgment. That, of course, makes Boisen neither unusual nor terribly dangerous; virtually every therapist has some difficulty with patients or clients who embody the therapist's own flaws.

Oscar lived 14 years after release until his death from cancer. During that time, he had one relapse during a period of enforced idleness but was assessed as "not insane." Boisen concluded that Oscar had given up everything for his wife, and that a rugged, self-reliant male would not find it easy to submit to such domination. Boisen was at least understanding and sympathetic on this issue. But to expect him to assist Oscar in valuing his own lust is to expect too much from Boisen; it was beyond his reach.

My view: both Rudolph and Oscar decompensated due to their anxiety over sex and their resulting submission to conventionally pious women. That is not to say that the women in question abused them; quite the contrary. Rudolph's and Oscar's abuse seems to have been mostly, if not entirely, introverted, rather than imposed from outside. And a driving force of it was their respective negativity about sexual pleasure. Where that inner conflict came from is not easily discovered. Perhaps it happened to them at the Revivals. Perhaps it was simply absorbed from pervasive Christian negativity about the libido embedded in Western culture at large.

We see in these two cases that Boisen, for all his brilliance, had significant myopia and debilitating repression in regards to sexual pleasure—that is, lust. On the one hand, he was an insightful assessor of the human psyche, but one who was by virtue of his own history uncomprehending about the place of the libido in life.

Boisen's life story demonstrates that one is limited by one's own personal history in what one can offer another person therapeutically. A person like Boisen, who seems never to have experienced interpersonal sexual pleasure and never thought he was entitled to it, cannot be expected to encase the value of that pleasure into his own integrated system. The value of physical sexual relations was simply an experience that was beyond Boisen's comprehension. And when he writes that sexual love must seek something more, beyond the object of desire, and cannot be satisfied with the finite, he is clearly in over his head, entering a world of fantasy. This was a major flaw in Boisen's writing, practice, theory, and vision of a psychologically healthy life. However, there is no such person as a perfect psychotherapist. We note that each of these two male patients was submissive to strong women, as was Boisen, who apparently was not skillful in working with persons who were that similar to him. But what therapist would be?

❖ ❖ ❖

In 1946, Abingdon-Cokesbury Press published a modest monograph by Boisen of some 30,000 words, awkwardly entitled *Problems in Religions and Life: A Manuel For Pastors,* subtitled *With Outlines for the Co-operative Study of Personal Experience in Social Situations.* [10] It was his third published monograph and written explicitly for the novice pastor. As Boisen put it, most curiously, in the Foreword:

"Relatively systematic study along the lines suggested in these pages will prove just as rewarding as the systematic study of books, and in many ways will be of more value in increasing the capacity of minister and church to build toward the Kingdom of God." [11]

Boisen, as an erudite polymath who was extremely well read in theology, psychology, sociology, and anthropology and widely published in journals of those fields as well, seems in this monograph to be turning his back on erudition in favor of the promotion of piety. His age of 70 may have also been against him.

This monograph consists of three parts. The Table of Contents is as follows:

Part One: Preliminary Studies: I. The Community; II. The Home and Its Members; III. The Individual and His Development.

Part Two: Types of Maladjustment: IV. The Mentally Ill; V. The Delinquent; VI. The Sexually Maladjusted; VII. The Alcoholic; VIII. The Physically Ill.

Part Three: General Problems: IX. Principles of Personal Counseling; X. Religious Education; XI. The Religious Conversion Experience Today; XII. The Religion of the Underprivileged; XIII. Moral Reconversion; XIV. Religion and Social Action; XV. The Distinctive Task of the Minister; XVI. The Minister's Library.

Curiously, at the end of each of the 16 very brief chapters, of about 2,500 words each, a short bibliography is listed. However, the bibliographies do not seem congruent with either the apparent intended readership or with the overall thesis of the monograph. Readers interested in the *Manual* would not likely turn to reading Freud, Jung, Malinowski, Horney, Rank, William Alanson White, and the like. Such reading cannot be expected of the rank beginners who seem to be the target of this monograph. And embarrassingly, Boisen's own *Exploration of the Inner World* is listed in seven separate suggested reading lists in this small monograph; hardly a capital crime, but it reflects the undisciplined character of the monograph itself. I found myself saddened that Boisen, who had done so much to radically redefine pastoral work in the twentieth century, was publishing so late in life such a pedestrian work; a work so out of step with his other writings and with the ambient culture as well.

The most dismaying part of the monograph is the six-page chapter entitled "The Sexually Maladjusted." Here, Boisen calls for the sex drive to be regulated, and that, most rigorously. "Organized religion has always been concerned with the regulation and interpretation of sex love," he wrote. The sins with which the evangelistic message has been concerned have largely been sexual transgressions, he argues, "and that quite properly." And further, "Sex love wants something which is beyond the finite love object." [12] The reader must wonder, "What, pray tell, do I lust for beyond the love object?" Boisen also objected to the challenge now being made to the right of the minister to deal with the problem of sex. This suggests that Boisen is getting some blow-back from his own teaching of sexual austerity. Self-mastery is Boisen's proposed cure to the problem of uncontrollable desires, which is to say *lust*. He seems oblivious to the great number of marginally potent persons who wish that they had more of those "uncontrollable desires." Then he expresses dismay that the real evil of masturbation has ominously been

HARRY STACK SULLIVAN AND ANTON T. BOISEN

forgotten, and furthermore, that sex indulgence is being divorced from the responsibilities of parenthood.

The only conclusion one can make of all this is that Boisen in his old age was regressing. And yet, still, he reports a visit with Sullivan in 1947, which he attests was very helpful to him. If Sullivan noted Boisen's decline, he would certainly have done everything he could to help Boisen maintain his own personal "security operations." But he would not have reported it to anyone. And Sullivan himself was also in decline physically, though apparently not mentally, and would live less than another two years.

❖ ❖ ❖

In 1950, Boisen published *Hymns of Hope and Courage*. [13] The hymnbook was specifically designed for use in psychiatric institutions. He culled the hymns in the Protestant tradition: those that were most likely, in his judgment, to spawn new psychotic episodes in psychiatric patients. Boisen in 1952 reprinted *The Exploration of the Inner World*, subsequent to Sullivan's death in January 1949. In a supplemental note in the Foreword of that edition, Boisen writes: "So far as concerns that body of organized and tested experience which is known as 'psychiatry,' it has therefore in large measure fallen by the wayside." [14] This is a vague and mysterious assertion, the meaning of which we can only conjecture. I venture to say that the comment is rooted in Boisen's unnamed grief at the loss of Sullivan, dead for three years at that point, and *fallen by the wayside* indeed. Boisen certainly was grieving his loss of any hope in finding a replacement for Sullivan in the world of psychiatry. And it must have been especially bitter to observe that the moguls of psychiatry were working overtime to obliterate Sullivan's name from history. With Sullivan's death, a large resource and fount of considerable wisdom went to the grave with him, and the effect on Boisen was likely devastating. To make matters worse, because Sullivan was transformed into

a non-person posthumously, Boisen was inhibited even from proclaiming in public the wisdom of Sullivan or his 25-year relationship with him.

❖ ❖ ❖

When the Council for Clinical Training (CCT) convened in Chicago in 1950 for its annual meeting and Twenty-Fifth Anniversary celebration, Boisen was invited to address the community, as was his due, since he was the founder of it all. Boisen began his clinical training program in 1925. Boisen's address was not well received by the community. His aging process had not treated him well. He was reverting to his life-long phobia over sexuality, embedded in him by his mother from his toddler years. The CPT community was already largely enamored by the Sexual Revolution. Boisen, the aging male, with a decade left to live was out of step with the community that he had created.

In his *Out of The Depths,* published in 1960, Boisen cited five paragraphs from his address to the gathered body at that time. He calls it his *credo.* Some excerpts: (The bold type here is my emphasis, not Boisen's.)

"...Even in the best of families and with the best of training ***unruly desires derived from our animal ancestry are likely to manifest themselves***. **The garden of the heart when left uncultivated is always taken over by weeds.**

"I believe that the real evil in functional mental illness is not to be found in discontent with one's imperfections, even when that discontent is carried to the point of severe disturbance, but in the sense of **estrangement and isolation due to the presence of instinctual claims which can neither be controlled nor acknowledged for fear of condemnation.** The aim of psychotherapy is not to ***get rid of the conflict by lowering the conscience threshold*** but to remove the sense of alienation by restoring the sufferer to the internalized fellowship of the best and thus setting him free to strive for his true objectives in life.

"... I believe that **the paramount human need is that for love and that there is a law within which forbids us to be satisfied with any fellowship save that of the best.**

"... From the religious standpoint the aim of education is to lead the growing individual to transfer his loyalty from the finite to the infinite and to recognize that his **parents are merely representatives of a higher loyalty, to which he owes unconditional allegiance**. For the religious man this loyalty is represented by his idea of God, and that idea stands for something which is operative in the lives of all men whether they recognize it or not. Ethical norms do not stand or fall with a belief in God, but they do not exist in a vacuum. They rest upon and are functions of the living relationships symbolized by such a belief, and they are validated by their long-run consequences in the lives of those who hold them." [15]

When Boisen named unruly animal desires and the presence of instinctual claims that cannot be controlled or acknowledged, his audience of pastoral clinicians knew exactly what he was alluding to. As an increasingly liberated group sexually, even before the emergence of the Sexual Revolution, Boisen's warning against sexual freedom would not have endeared him at that point to most of the members of the community he founded.

Boisen at this point in his life was a man approaching his eighth decade, who was yet to understand the pathology in his mother's panicky rush to have him circumcised at age four. He was an instrument of psychotherapy for multitudes but found little of it for himself.

His 1950 report to the community further exposed Boisen's decline. He had the right, and the authority, to claim the value of what he had almost singlehandedly created: the clinical pastoral movement and its assertion of a clear alliance with psychiatry. Such a claim was explicitly supported by Harry Stack Sullivan. Certainly, Helen Flanders Dunbar, also a psychiatrist, was a crucial and essential ally who kept Boisen afloat until early in the 1940s, when she was dismissed from her position of authority in the Council for Clinical Training for political reasons. (She also experienced other terrible personal blows, and in 1959 she finally, tragically drowned in her basement swimming pool.) What Boisen had created, primarily with Dunbar's strong support in the first decade and a half, was monumental, changing the shape of American Protestantism and, ultimately, American religion. He could not have done it without Dunbar. This was the achievement Boisen should have addressed in his likely final appearance before the assembled clinical pastoral community that was allegedly implementing his vision. But instead, he reverted to exegeting his struggle with sexual pleasure and the demands the bourgeois sexual ethics put on him and were indeed internalized by him. In his declining years, as Boisen increasingly regressed becoming even more his mother's boy, he was also increasingly ignored by his presumptive disciples and comrades.

❖ ❖ ❖

In an article published in *Pastoral Psychology* after Boisen's death, Menninger Clinic psychologist Paul Pruyser recounted a meeting with Boisen, held sometime in Boisen's latter years. It seems by then that Boisen had decompensated further. We can assume that his deficits were heightened with age and relative isolation as well as, perhaps, his bout with another rumored schizophrenic episode. There is some irony in the fact that the man who brought such profound psychiatric enlightenment to the world of religion, literally inventing "pastoral psychotherapy," seemed to deteriorate psychologically in his old age.

Quoting Paul Pruyser:

"The most outstanding feature of the man at the time I knew him was his flat affect. There is an awful psychiatric expression referring to chronic schizophrenic patients, who have made a good hospital adjustment, or sometimes have been discharged and live on the outside. That expression is 'burned out case.' This phrase came into my mind time and time again when I talked with [Boisen] and saw him act. He was not without humor and delicacy, but something had happened to his feelings and their expression.

"He was very courteous to me, interested in some of my thoughts, and whether he himself talked about pleasant or unpleasant things in his life, it was all stated in the same monotonous, deliberately affect-free language. He also had a faraway look. Yet I must say that there was something very likable about the man, perhaps in part because of the tragic stamp on his life. I have always felt that his *Out of The Depths,* which came out a year or so later, conveys in its tone and selection of topics exactly the impression I gained in my personal confrontation with him. The language is beautiful, the topics are moving, but there is something utterly pathetic about it all. There is something of homesickness in it, ennobled by a sense of suffering. In his presence I felt respect towards him, because of the cross he had to bear. But it was difficult to warm up towards him for there was an odd distance between himself and the rest of the world. I also felt at that time that he knew he was dying, slowly and with several ups and downs physically, so that one felt somehow in the presence of a man preparing himself for death. This certainly augmented my sense of reverence towards him, but again, made it difficult for me to invest myself in him." [16]

❖ ❖ ❖

In 1960, Boisen published *Out of The Depths*, his autobiography. It is a remarkable account of his life, complete with his five psychotic episodes. (He was said to have had a sixth sometime later, in the early 1960s.) There is no record of when Boisen actually wrote the book, but we can assume that it was mostly written sometime earlier; likely much earlier. Given the highly personal data included, Boisen perhaps assumed that it might be used to embarrass him in the workplace. As he was in the process of negotiating with the publisher, Boisen was on the receiving end of strong protests from his sister who opposed disclosure of accounts of embarrassing sexual data from the family archives. The publisher apparently came close to rejecting the book because of pressure from the sister to delete so much material. Somehow, Boisen, the family, and the publisher reached common ground after some deletions. The information that was excised would be interesting to know, but at this point in history, the chances of discovering it are slim to none. *Out of The Depths* is the most edifying literary monument that Boisen left to mankind. If the family had succeeded in repressing the book altogether, it would have been a great loss for world literature.

Subsequent to the death of Sullivan, Boisen lived another 16 years, but the final years left him increasingly debilitated, and mostly alone. He was living in complementary—and poorly maintained—housing next to the kitchen at Elgin State Hospital in Chicago, in a storage room with only a screen door. The hospital fed and sheltered him, but obviously not very well, especially considering his decades of service there. By the time Boisen died at Elgin in 1965 at age 89, Harry Stack Sullivan was all but forgotten in the clinical pastoral movement, and for the most part, in the world of psychiatry as well. It was not long before Boisen, too, would be mostly forgotten. His name still lingers, even today, in the several organizations of the clinical pastoral movement; but what he achieved in life, what he represented, his transformation of American religion, have all become, generally speaking, a lost memory.

The emerging sexual revolution further separated Boisen from those who were committed to the clinical pastoral training agenda that Boisen himself had created. Most pastoral clinicians welcomed the sexual revolution as a long-hoped-for movement toward personal freedom and an affirmation of sexual pleasure. Sullivan, had he lived, would have rejoiced to see that day. Boisen blessedly died just as the Sexual Revolution was making its appearance.

We have to ask why both Sullivan and Boisen were so totally forgotten in the brief period after their deaths. The public amnesia directed at them was different in each case. The memory of Sullivan was massively repressed in the world of psychology; likely payback for all the glass he broke in his life. However, his legacy lived on in multiple varied forms of schools in psychology. His ghost remains strong, continuing to shape the various iterations of psychology and its attention to the interpersonal as complementary to the unconscious and to Freud. In a profound sense, Sullivan won the day, but won anonymously; psychiatry became, in large part, a profession of ingrates.

The amnesia related to Boisen was quite different, a reverse image to that of Sullivan. His name continued to be trumpeted by the various organizations claiming to carry forth the work of his clinical pastoral training. But very few of his heirs remembered the substance of Boisen's revolution or continued to embody the theory and practice of his pastoral psychotherapy. That work was drowned out by the noise of "religion, spirituality and prayer." Thus, Boisen arguably fared worse than Sullivan. Better to have the unattributed substance of one's creativity carried forth to future generations; the name can easily be resurrected later and reattached with ease. But when the substance is washed out, reconstruction requires yet another revolution. The Boisen movement—that is, the clinical pastoral training movement—is currently, with few exceptions, an empty shell, a form without substance.

Psychiatry will have to answer eventually for the disappearing act that it inflicted on Harry Stack Sullivan; but since Sullivan is dead, there is no need to rush. His massive written and recorded record will likely remain intact until some critical mass of psychotherapists takes a closer look at his life and work. Pastoral clinicians will have more to answer for, namely the obliteration of Boisen's substantive and critical contribution.

❖ ❖ ❖

Henry Nouwen personally visited Anton Boisen at Elgin a year before Boisen's death. Nouwen was a devotee of Boisen, though data suggests that he did not really understand him. Harry Stack Sullivan's name did not come up in Nouwen's account of that visit. But Freud's name was broached, and Boisen emphatically declared his indebtedness to Freud. One might argue that Boisen was indebted even more to Sullivan than to Freud, both theoretically and personally over a quarter-century. If history could be reenacted, Nouwen should have been instructed to ask Boisen what Sullivan meant to him. However, Boisen was said to be exhibiting evidence of some degree of dementia and may not have been capable of a cogent answer. And, in deference to Nouwen, the visit seems to have been more a social one than a pursuit of historical data. [17]

In the pastoral community, one might think that the Boisen-Sullivan relationship would have been seen as a trophy—an authentically great victory—supporting the therapeutic competence of clinically trained pastors. And indeed, in some corners that was the case, at least indirectly, as in the Wayne Oates and Myron Madden network, the Southern Baptist Association for Clinical Pastoral Education. However, in the clinical pastoral movement as a whole, the tide was moving against the pastoral clinician as psychotherapist and towards the pastoral clinician as a *spiritual* resource and prayer warrior. We have reached mean low tide, as exemplified in the works of George Fitchett and others of his persuasion, for whom the pastoral clinician is a religious cheerleader, the farthest thing conceivable from a pastoral psychotherapist.

By the end of his life, Boisen had become an icon without content. Pastoral clinicians praised his name for the next half century without having the slightest idea of what he accomplished and without having read a word he wrote. Such results are in part Boisen's fault. He failed to claim the ground he had won in his relationship with Sullivan and the credibility it gave him. But he was only one man, and one man can accomplish only so much. Thus, the theoretical victory of the clinical pastoral training movement 70 years ago has turned to ashes, and the struggle must be begun again. But thanks both to Boisen's genius as well as his flaws, pastoral clinicians will know better how to succeed next time.

---

1. Judges, 11:29:40, p. 285, *The New English Bible with The Apocrypha,* Oxford University Press, 1970.

2. Boisen, Anton T. *Out of The Depths: An Autobiographical Study of Mental Disorder and Religious Experience.* New York: Harper & Brothers, Publishers, 1960, p. 206. (Hereafter, OTD.)

3. Ibid., p. 192, and personal communication.

4. *Out of the Depths, op. cit.,* p. 186., also p. 199.

5. Ibid., 183–4.

6. Chicago Theological Seminary Library, archival letter file for Anton Boisen.

7. Boisen, Anton T. *Religion in Crisis and Culture: A Sociological and Psychological Study.* New York: Harper & Brothers Publishers, 1945, pp. 52–53.

8. Ibid.

9. Ibid., p. 58.
10. Boisen, Anton T. *Problems in Religions and Life: A Manuel For Pastors,* subtitled *With Outlines for the Co-operative Study of Personal Experience in Social Situations.*
11. Ibid., Foreword, p. 8.
12. Boisen, *Problems in Religion and Life. op.cit.,* p. 75.
13. Boisen, Anton T. *Hymns of Hope and Courage.* 1950.
14. Boisen, *The Exploration of the Inner World*, 1949 edition, Author's Note to 1952 Edition, p. x.
15. OTD, pp. 196–7.
16. Pruyser, Paul. (September, 1966). "Anton T. Boisen and Theology Through Living Human Documents." Henry J. M. Nouwen, *Pastoral Psychology*, pp. 49-50.
17. Henri J. M. Nouwen Legacy Trust, Sally Keeefe Cohen, Literary Manager, John M. Kelly Library University of St. Michaels College, 113 St. Joseph's Street, Toronto, Ontario, Canada, MSS 114. (Note: Some readers have confused the "Sullivan" who was then Chaplain of Elgin with Harry Stack Sullivan.)

CHAPTER 8

Sullivan On Sexuality

∽∞∾

Sullivan's marquee assertion on the subject of sexuality did not put him in a class with Lord Byron and the other high romantics. He famously wrote: "Sex is important for the twenty minutes it may occupy from time to time, but it is not necessarily behind everything else that fills the rest of the time." [1] Nor did this assertion endear him to the Hollywood cult of romantic love, where sexual pleasure is seemingly the goal and purpose of everything worth living for. In just one sentence, Sullivan stamped *fini* on dreams of perpetual eroticism and romanticism as the goal and purpose of the human experience. On the other hand, Sullivan may have been the most sexually liberated and liberating of psychotherapists of his generation—or perhaps, ever. Or, he was simply the only one with courage enough to speak the unvarnished truth on a subject about which very few dared even to whisper a candid word: the place of sexual pleasure in human life, and the acceptable boundaries thereof.

As a corollary, Sullivan burst the illusory American balloon of coitus as the purpose of marriage; perhaps the only culture in human history to nurture such fantasies. Still further, Sullivan by implication removed coitus from the control of state, secular, or religious authorities as much by the example of his life as by what he wrote. However, no one can be certain exactly what Sullivan's own personal sexual practices were, as if that mattered. While he left many hints, he seems to have maintained absolute privacy on the subject of what he might have done, if anything, to satisfy his own lust. And with good reason: being unmarried for life, any data about him regarding his sexual habits would have been a public relations threat. Apparently, he was determined to survive in Twentieth-century America, Inc.

Sullivan was never more radical than when he unambiguously and boldly declared not only the legitimacy of *lust*, but also by proclaiming the necessity of acknowledging one's own *lust dynamism*, as he called it, for those who aimed for mental health. Refreshingly, Sullivan gave lust its rightful and dignified place in the human experience. Genital lust, he assured us, is not love, but merely a felt need for genital pleasure. Neither, according to Sullivan, is lust the most promising entry into a relationship of life-long intimacy. It is simply what it is, *the human need for genital pleasure*. It appears to be a universal experience of all animal life, without which a species would not endure, and, in the case of homo sapiens—according Sullivan—one's mental health deteriorates if one is denied the satisfaction of lust.

Furthermore, an erotic-lustful relationship may or may not mature into a reciprocally loving, caring, and permanent relationship, such as marriage or partnership. Sullivan suggested that people need to build caring and enduring relationships that are prepared to survive the waxing and waning of lust, and even survive the ultimate disappearance of lust altogether. To put it plainly, Sullivan distinguished lust from long-term caring relationships, such as marriage. A parallel problem, in the American culture particularly, is that persons pursue the need for genital pleasure unreflectively. Thus they consequently trap themselves in marriages founded *once upon a time* on lust and lust alone. Such marriages likely have a short half-life. On the other hand, a marriage founded on both love and lust "may survive indefinitely the loss of sexual satisfactions." It may even survive the integration of sexual satisfaction with persons not in the marital relationship." [2]

Of all the cultures known to history, certainly Western Christian cultural practices of sexuality and marriage—the American iteration being the most extreme—are the most oblivious to Sullivan's claim. Unlike people in many other cultures, Western Christians generally marry out of lust. As lust wanes, alienation typically arrives. Then the marriage disintegrates. Hence the high divorce rate. Many other cultures understand Sullivan's thesis: that the lust drive and the creation of a permanent, caring relationship, such as marriage, are separate agendas requiring separate assessments and separate expectations. These cultures are more successful in maintaining marital stability.

Sullivan makes very clear that interpersonal intimacy is the essential foundation for mental health. But he is also clear that the lust drive must be satisfied, and that the risks of repressing it are potentially dire for one's mental health. Furthermore, genital lust satisfaction does not necessarily result in significant interpersonal intimacy; it is simply a human need that must be satisfied, like air, food, and water. Prostitutes have understood this since the beginning of history but, for many reasons, Hollywood never has. The American romantic ideal—as portrayed in our literature, theater, and film—seems to assume and imply that all forms of lust must be attended by bells, whistles, total self-sacrificial devotion, and ultimately, lifelong marriage. But according to Sullivan, the satisfaction of the demands of lust and the wish to create a stable and permanent loving relationship are two separate tracks that some may find congruent, but probably most will not. The two needs are radically different and require radically different behavioral responses. Jews have understood this through history; Catholics and most other Christians never have.

Those teachers and writers who promoted a more liberated sexuality in the West during the 1960s Sexual Revolution had unknowingly been preempted by Sullivan by several decades, actually from the grave. He laid the philosophical foundation for the Sexual Revolution a generation prior to the actual Revolution. But no one was reading Sullivan then, and no one to speak of is reading him now. The leaders of the Revolution might have been more potent if they had studied Sullivan in advance...if they could have found his works. They then might have used Sullivan as an authority to proclaim the great value of the Revolution to mental health. Perhaps they understood that it was not simply an opportunity to free people of a burden but actually was contributing vitally to overall mental health in the culture at large in asserting that the repression of lust is extremely dangerous to one's mental health. Unhappily, Sullivan died too soon. But as he himself put it: "The point which I wish to emphasize now is that, late as it is in maturing, the genital lust dynamism is something that can be dissociated only at grave risk to effective living, and in most people it cannot be dissociated at all. It will again and again, at whatever great expense to security, whatever suffering from anxiety, manifest itself." [3] Sullivan, the Catholic boy born into mystical libido-negating late nineteenth-century rural New York State, and in the context of a rabid right-wing soul-saving Protestant culture, became the most powerful nemesis ever for Christian ethics—both Catholic and Protestant—since Augustine of Hippo. [4]

Sullivan also broke glass in the land of those who cherish the widely lauded mutual orgasm. He wrote: "In metagenital situations one's [own] genitals need not play a part, as in masturbating another person, or fellatio." [5] In other words, helping a friend satisfy a drive for genital pleasure does not require satisfaction in the other; the dream or ideal of mutual orgasm is overrated. Once again, wise prostitutes and "madams" have known this from time immemorial. The long and short of all this is that Sullivan predicted emotional and perhaps psychiatric distress for anyone who attempts to deny to him or herself the pleasures derived from lust. And the counterpoint to this, at least in this infantile American culture, is social disgrace for anyone who makes public his or her actions in pursuit of the demands of lust. [6]

Sullivan continued: "Many of the people I saw as mental patients might have been more fortunate in their adolescence had they carried on their preliminary heterosexual experimentation with a good-natured prostitute, as compared to what they actually experienced. The number of wretched experiences connected with adolescents' first heterosexual attempts are legion." [7]

Sullivan argued that the Western world has plenty of elaborate apparatuses for inhibiting integration or inclusion of lust into what he calls *the self-system:* a Sullivanian neologism, which seems to be a replacement, more or less, for the Freudian ego and the id, or in Freud's German: *Das Ich und das Es.* Sullivan had a practice of supplanting Freudian language with a language of his own. No one can be faulted for that if one can get away with it, and in fact, "the self-system" may be a more appropriate and earthy label than "ego," "id," and "superego." As wise as he was, none of Freud's identifying labels have divine sanction. Since Sullivan understood ego as completely dependent on affirming interpersonal relationships, the concept of self-system may communicate more clearly "the self in relationship" than "ego" does in relation to other aspects of one's personality. In any case, there is nothing sacred about such labels. So the self-system seems to refer to the way we authorize the things we believe and the things we do, or the way we give credit for who we are. Sullivan seems to say that the self-system is formed in the infant from pain, fear, and anxiety, though he later said that both approbation and disapproval shape the self-system. Sullivan was always cautious about undermining the patient's self-system.

To accomplish his new value system, Sullivan asserted, "we must set up what are, so far as I know, unique inventions: the resolute separation of the need for intimacy from the requirements of lust." He added, furthermore, "that how fatuous it is to toss out adjectives like heterosexual, homosexual, and narcissistic to classify a person as to his sexual and friendly integrations with others. Such classifications are nowhere near refined enough for

147

intelligent thought; they are much too gross to do anything but mislead both the observer and the victim. For example, to talk about homosexuality's being a problem really means about as much as to talk about humanity's being a problem…and by lust I don't mean some great striving libido or what not. **By lust I mean simply the felt aspect of the genital drive.**" (Emphasis mine.) [8] Sullivan insisted that schizophrenic psychosis "seems never to occur in those who have achieved if only for a short time a definitely satisfying adjustment to a sex object." [9]

Sullivan elaborated on the ubiquitous collisions between one's lust and one's security operations in the American middle class. By *security operations,* a phrase Sullivan often employs, he meant one's feelings of self-esteem, personal worth, and comfort in social contexts. In the American middle class, exposure to others of one's own libidinal needs can be socially fatal and result in a profound loss of *security.* The typical middle-class American is as horny, or sexually "turned on," as people are in any other cultural context, but Americans are monumentally, endemically, and neurotically secretive about it. Survival requires secrecy.

Repressive pressures on the libido come from many directions. According to Sullivan, many parents simply do not want their children to become adults who are interested in *such things as sex.* Sensitive administrators in the workplace will quake at the slightest evidence of libido making an appearance in the office. The pervasive anxiety in American middle-class culture over issues of sexuality seeps into all aspects of human relationships. It sets up adolescents for wretched experiences related to an adolescent's first attempts at sexual pleasure. The accounts are legion. [10]

Many males are also vexed by the precocious or premature orgasm in their first heterosexual attempts; a phenomenon of no actual consequence, or as Sullivan puts it, "with about as much significance as drinking a glass of water." [11] As a consequence, the first sexual experiences in American culture are often accompanied by guilt, shame, aversion, or revulsion, making it problematic for the pair involved to care for each other, as if they had been party to a disgraceful act. These are not very blessed attributes to possess while learning how to live with one's lust in the world as it is, said Sullivan.

It seems that in Sullivan's view, the sublimation of lust to more socially acceptable goals is an ominous splitting of the human experience. To illustrate, he wrote, "We have a prolongation and refinement of the separation of good and bad girls." The one view is that all women are good—too good; they are noble, and one cannot approach them for anything so *something-or-other* as genital satisfaction. And on the other hand, there is the view that all women are extremely unattractive, unsuited to anything but a particular kind of hateful entanglement, which becomes practically official business in the satisfaction of lust.

In this one paragraph, Sullivan would appear to diagnose *in absentia* Anton Boisen's libidinal conflict (along with, arguably, most of the males in twentieth-century America). Boisen thought he had found, in Alice Batchelder, his dream woman, but one who seemingly would not tolerate in any respect becoming the object of Boisen's lust, and in that regard, also fit Boisen's value system perfectly. Boisen's libido had been on maternally enforced lockdown since he was a toddler. That neurosis, of course, did not prevent Sullivan from appreciating what Boisen contributed to the world. No one is perfect.

Sullivan continued on the subject of "difficulties to which man is heir... in which there are covert processes not accessible to awareness (unconscious processes, to use the old-fashioned term) which are attended by pseudo-heterosexual practices with or without an attenuation of the contact with members of the same sex. This sort of thing is often a precursor of a lifelong course of searching for the 'ideal' woman or man, with the recurrent discovery of serious imperfections in each candidate...a classical field for the appearance of extremely unpleasant jealousy...which is very close to providing an adequate picture of the now old-fashioned Christian hell.

149

Plenty of instances in which these people either set up housekeeping, or go through the motions of marrying, and even have children, but mostly for security reasons." [12]

Sullivan drove home his argument:

"Precautionary activities enable us to conceal the fact that we are motivated by lust, and tend to protect us from very brutally making fools of ourselves. It is impossible for us to make a statement that lust is present. Any denizen of the Western world has plenty of elaborate apparatuses for inhibiting integration in the interest of lust, when such interrelation would collide with the self-system. Everyone may remember times when he was singularly restless and uncomfortable with the unrecognized presence of lust; and this lust was unrecognized not because it is hard to know lust, but because there was some powerful impulse active to inhibit its recognition. The culture is so very hard on consensual validation and syntactic operations with respect to lust. Our culture is the least adequate in preparing one for meeting the eventualities of sexual maturity, which is another way of saying we are the most sex-ridden people on the face of the globe." [13]

Sullivan contended that one must attend to the suitability of the situation for probable satisfaction. There are often factors that might make the suitability of satisfaction less than promising, and might make lustful excitement strangely irrelevant. He pointed out, for example, the unwisdom of getting intensely sexually excited about one's opponent in traffic court. [14]

Precautionary activities enable us to conceal the fact that we are motivated by lust and tend to protect us from making fools of ourselves. The Western world has many devices to inhibit the integration of lust into human lives. There is a powerful impulse abroad to inhibit its recognition, said Sullivan. What he did not say is that the principal religion of the Western world, Christianity, is the driving force of that inhibition. Lust is first on the list of the so-called "seven deadly sins." On the other hand, Judaism, the mother religion of both Christianity and Islam, acknowledges the legitimacy of lust (as does Islam). One cannot read the Jewish religious texts without a stunning awareness that sex is better than good, and that if there is a God, he or she wants everyone to enjoy the pleasures of sex in all its fullness, and preferably on the holiest day of the week, the Sabbath. Rahab the Harlot is notable as a biblical woman who is explicitly identified as a woman of both faith and virtue. Quite an achievement for a *whore*. [15] Of course, Jews within the cultural contexts of Christian nations generally lie low on such matters, rightly seeking to avoid the next pogrom. From Sullivan's perspective, the lust dynamism must be integrated into the self-system in order to maintain psychological health. But our culture is the least adequate in preparing persons for such sexual maturity and integration. [16]

Sullivan also challenged the sacred cow of monogamy. He contended that "children cared for by groups of more than two adults decidedly have the better chance of successful personality growth." [17] No one, certainly no psychiatrist, not even Wilhelm Reich, has contributed more to the ideology of sexual freedom than Sullivan.

Sullivan was generally contemptuous of the sexual skills of mature American men, of whom he saw a great many. He characterized their sexual practices generally as "masturbation via vagina." Sullivan lifted that metaphor from his early mentor, the psychiatrist Edward J. Kempf, to whom he was indebted in many other respects as well. Sullivan wrote that he encountered innumerable husbands who masturbate through the instrumentality of their wives' vaginas and feel much more adult than they would using only their hands. They have failed, said Sullivan, to develop authentic heterosexual interests; the deficiency often lies in a failure of elaborating a differentiation from the primitive mother sentiment. It seems that Sullivan is warning women that if they want good sex in a relationship with a man, they should avoid getting close to a *mama's boy,* a man who cannot differentiate himself from the primitive mother sentiment. A mama's boy will not attend to what he can do to gratify his sexual partner, but merely to how he can please himself. Hence the characterization, *"masturbate via vagina."* [18]

Sullivan was equally contemptuous of parents who react to a boy's nocturnal emissions with something on the order of "this must not happen again." As long as wet dreams, or sex in any form, are "a thing of darkness and shame, and one of our most cherished cultural depravities, the infection of adolescents with venereal diseases and syphilitic disintegration of brain tissue will continue." (Sullivan had a marvelous way of verbally taking no prisoners.) Congruent with his posture on sexuality, Sullivan reported that he replied to a patient who made sexual overtures to him, "I know I would enjoy it, but it would gum up the work terribly and the work is more important.... I am selling an expert service and not having a good time." [19] Whether he was addressing a male patient or a woman is not stated, and actually matters not. Sullivan's practical, down to earth, and non-romantic posture toward sexual pleasure is quite refreshing, and an excellent antidote to Hollywood and American culture in general, but also an antidote to Boisen's quite conventional, and oppressive, sexual inhibitions and restraints, rooted in virtually all manifestations of Christianity. The reader can hear between the lines—and sometimes even *within* the lines—the delight Sullivan took in ridiculing American middle-class sexual mores, *viz* "cultural conventions that make us the most sex-ridden people of whom I have any knowledge." [20]

Sullivan engaged in a long peroration on the fate of the male child in the crib. The hands of the male child, he says, will fall upon a small protuberance in the groin. The mother will then take it upon herself to organize the infant on the basis of our more rigid puritanical tradition. She will feel that Satan is in the very near vicinity, and that "here is a manifestation of the bestial nature of man in the very act of erupting in her infant, and will want to do something about it. She will want to save this infant...the stress on the mother is terrific." The doctor is consulted, and the doctor is very anxious to build up a good practice and surmises that this mother will bring him other patients... so he puts medical "intelligence" to work. So the infant has a mitten put on the offending hand with an attachment tied around the waist. [21]

Sullivan went on:

"But immobilization of the right hand does not immobilize the left. Presently both hands are immobilized, and by this time even an infant begins to realize that all this has something to do with his genitals.... When I was younger and more reckless about language, I called that state a 'primary genital phobia,' that is, an irrational fear of the genitalia.

"And so here we have a person who, long before puberty, has come to have considerable conflict of impulse pertaining to genital manipulation. Of course, one is always waking up to discover that one has violated this regulation in one's sleep.... One has the feeling, 'Oh the devil that is in me. Here I am, doing this worst of possible things in my sleep.'" [22]

Sullivan registered a warning to fellow psychiatrists: if we cannot find something besides the sexual problem in strangers who come to us for help, we will be useless as therapists. Quite often, he argued, the sexual difficulty is remedied in the process of dealing with other problems. What Sullivan meant by this is that a person who develops a clear personal identity and an ability to stand on his or her own will not be intimidated by the neurotic pressures of the ambient culture, especially its profound cultural confusion and conflict over the place of sexual pleasure in life. In closing, Sullivan added a vast understatement: "You may notice that there is a slight difference here between my views and some of the views that have been circulated in historic times." [23] As a kind of grace note, Sullivan added that the highly civilized Chinese of the pre-Christian era were not bowled over by sex. Nor were many other cultures, particularly primitive ones. [24]

Note: It remains a mystery as to what these two great men, Boisen and Sullivan, did with their respectively discordant sexual views in their congenial and mutually affirming quarter-century relationship. I suspect that Sullivan simply understood Boisen's origins and history, and gave him a pass on the issue. Likely, he understood Boisen's crippling upbringing, major parts from which he never recovered, but that is a mere guess. However Sullivan assessed Boisen, he probably realized that Boisen compensated for his delusions about the meaning of sex with reality-based patient work in other arenas. Clearly, Sullivan held Boisen in considerable esteem, in spite of his particular manifestations of his craziness.

Now it is perhaps clear why Sullivan throughout his professional life was strongly averse to the public media and remained in the media closets, so to speak, sticking mainly to private practice and a small group of like-minded fellow practitioners. If he had emerged in popular culture and gotten the attention of say, Walter Winchell, or some other shrill media mogul who might have disseminated the details of his radicalism, the negative consequences for Sullivan are not hard to imagine.

In summary, Harry Stack Sullivan was explicitly the most radical of all psychotherapists in consistently promoting sexual liberation; no one else can touch him. He insisted that, at risk to our psychological health, lust must be assuaged. No other *curer of souls* has dared to be so courageous and so correct. At the same time, he was the most radical of psychotherapists in placing lust in its proper place, as *secondary* to the satisfactions of *interpersonal intimacy*. If this radical Sullivanian reordering of our sexual values could be universalized, our current, sexually sick, Hollywood-drenched culture might enter a new golden age of relative mental health. If indeed Sullivan *was* homosexual or bisexual, as is rumored, it would be ironic that it took a social and sexual outcast to understand most profoundly the gift of human sexuality, and courageously, at great risk to himself personally, to boldly propose a radical reordering of our thinking about sexual pleasure.

II

In Sullivan's therapeutic writing on homosexuality, he asserted that preadolescent homosexual experiences are generally to be expected, are not to be considered abnormal, and that they usually prepare the way for the later, more mature heterosexual relationships. The goal must be to dissolve the patient's barrier to intimacy with the other gender. In that sense, he saw preadolescent homosexuality as positive and developmentally healthy. Furthermore, he left open entirely the question of whether such a relationship would be genitally consummated; he wrote as if it mattered not. Without saying so directly, he seemed to suggest that it would be beneficial. The evidence shows, wrote Sullivan, that overt homosexuality in adolescent gangs, genitally consummated or not, does not inhibit, but rather even enhances heterosexual development in maturity. But Sullivan does not suggest in any way that he was writing this as autobiography.[25]

In his work with patients, Sullivan seemed not to have accepted any bold and blanket claims from a patient confessing to be homosexual. "If a patient says, 'You know I am a homosexual,' I say, 'Well, I don't know what you mean by homosexual? It had not occurred to me. What do you mean by homosexual? This queer idea that you are a homosexual....'" Sullivan is, of course, making a humorous play on words here with the injection of "queer idea." He is cleverly, and playfully, saying, "You think you're queer, do you, but your self-diagnosis is actually what seems queer."[26]

Sullivan described in detail how he engaged a patient around issues of sexuality:

"After certain oddly confusing motions by a patient, which I have learned usually means that 'A Great Problem' is about to be revealed, and after considerable delay at which I finally show some slight impatience, he may say: 'Well, I have a sexual problem.' Since I suspect at this rate we'll get nowhere in an hour and a half, I may say, 'And doubtless a homosexual problem.' The patient may then say, 'Yes, Doctor, that's it.' I may learn that he has often had sexual relations with members of his own sex, or that he has been unable to think of having relations with a member of the other sex, or *something*. That's what this homosexual problem means to me—just *something*. The real problem which I hope finally to uncover, to my patient's satisfaction, and with his clear insight, is what stands in the way of his making the conventional, and therefore the comparatively simple adjustment, which is regarded as normal. In other words, I don't treat any alleged entities such as homosexuality." [27]

Sullivan was making the point that when you encounter a person with "a homosexual problem," what counts is what you discover about that person. "Quite often that leads you back to the early years. I've never found myself called upon to 'cure' anybody. The patient takes care of that once I clear away the brush." [28]

While Sullivan was explicitly tolerant, and even affirming, of preadolescent physical homosexuality, he seemed not so affirming of adult homosexuality, at least in his theory. If Sullivan was indeed an adult practicing homosexual, as many seem to think, he did not wear his sexual orientation like a badge of honor, but rather like something not to be discussed in public. He wrote: "I have come to recognize [adult] homosexuality as a developmental mistake, dictated by the culture as a substitute behavior in those instances in which the person cannot do what is the simplest thing to do. Thus I try to find out why he can't do the simplest thing...." [29]

Sullivan's own works reflect a man who was quite relaxed and self-assured about his own personal sexual identity, whatever it consisted of, and therefore in turn relaxed about the sexuality of others as well. And one gets a similar impression on reading Helen Swick Perry's biography of him. Such a stance will not be any comfort to those *political* homosexuals who strive to enhance the public and social standing of homosexuality as a social entity. If one has a wooden leg, then one simply has a wooden leg. Why do we need to declare it to be "normal?" Sullivan seems to be saying: It is what it is; not to be mocked, not to be lauded, simply accepted as part of the human drama; not to be punished; not to be championed.

On the other hand, we cannot rule out the possibility that Sullivan was labeling homosexuality in maturity a failure in order to protect himself politically in relation to the vicious homophobic culture. It would make a strong line of defense were he himself to be publicly charged. Sullivan was no dummy.

On one issue Sullivan was consistently unambiguous: he insisted that intimacy was neither primarily nor exclusively genital. As he put it so *sullivanianly,* "Some people imagine that intimacy is only a matter of approximating genitals one to another." [30]

III

The question of Sullivan's own personal sexual practice has been a subject over which much hysteria erupted, and many unsubstantiated claims have been asserted. A number of writers in recent decades have taken to referring to the "gay Sullivan," as if Sullivan's homosexuality was an established fact.

Carlton Cornett, in an otherwise useful monograph published in 2018, wrote: "Though it has been debated for decades, it is beyond doubt that Harry Stack Sullivan was gay." [31] But Cornett does not cite a single piece of hard data to support his contention. And when he cites Robert G. Kvarnes, who knew Sullivan personally over many years, as his supporting data, his citation is a misquote. Kvarnes actually wrote that while many have thought Sullivan to be homosexual, "I don't know of any instances of acknowledged homosexual relationships."[32]

Cornett's claim—and that of the many others who concur—is a bridge too far, reporting only intuitions that are unsubstantiated. At the end of the day, no one can say at this point in time with confidence exactly what Sullivan did to gratify himself sexually. Sullivan certainly communicated by innuendo that he was a person of sexual experience. He never married, therefore whatever gratification he found was non-marital. But whether or not he was a practicing homosexual is simply a question, the answer to which is out of reach.

Any conclusive identification of Sullivan as "gay" is both invasive and anachronistic—and certainly unsubstantiated. Tangentially, that Sullivan would permit himself to be labeled as a "gay" *anything* is inconceivable. He could be relentlessly obstreperous on most any subject, more especially those that gained popular currency in the wider culture. If he were alive today, I doubt he would allow himself to be referred to in such terms without leveling either a vicious counterattack or a stony silence. And Sullivan could be both stonily silent and verbally vicious!

The actual situation here is that there is a great deal of *circumstantial* evidence for supporting the view of a "homosexual Sullivan," and while the bulk of it creates a very weighty argument, all of the amassed "evidence" fails to provide clear and certain support for Sullivan as a homosexual. And that is a real problem for those who wish to identify him *conclusively* as homosexual.

We do know by his own account that Sullivan developed a significant prepubescent relationship with his neighbor, Clarence Bellinger, who was five years older than Sullivan. But we do not have many details. What little that is known is that the friendship began when Sullivan was eight, and Bellinger, thirteen. The friendship seems to have been close; Sullivan writes as though it saved his life psychologically in his latency period. Bellinger was the only person who was anything close to being a peer friend in Sullivan's socially isolated preadolescence. For some period of time, they rode in a horse-drawn wagon to school, and their relationship was very positive, if not lifesaving. Though five years his senior, Bellinger graduated and left for college only two years prior to Sullivan's own graduation. There is no record of their seeing each other again. But at some point, the relationship became acrimonious, with Bellinger later in life referring to Sullivan as a "homosexual and a son-of-a-bitch." [33]

As for his accusation that Sullivan was a son-of-a-bitch, Bellinger could have found many witnesses who would have supported that charge. But the charge of homosexuality has as yet no corroboration. It is plausible that Bellinger and Sullivan themselves engaged in genital sexual relations. It is noteworthy that Sullivan considered such a preadolescent relationship normal and indeed potentially therapeutic, whether genitally acted out or not, and even useful psychologically in moving toward the *desired* heterosexuality. However, whatever the physical make-up of their relationship, Sullivan considered his youthful friendship with Bellinger to have been salvific. He viewed preadolescent homosexual bonding, whether genital or not, to be essential to mature development in post-adolescence. But what Sullivan and Bellinger may have done with each other sexually speaking is simply not known. How, when, and why their relationship went on the rocks has never been determined. [34]

According to Sullivan, the appropriate goal in the prepubescent developmental stage, the "homosexual stage," must be the ultimate dissolving of the patient's barrier to full intimacy with persons of the other sex. Unfortunately we do not have personal data on either Sullivan or Bellinger (except rumors of their homosexuality) as to how they may have transitioned into full homo- or heterosexual puberty, if they did. Both men became psychiatrists; Bellinger a far less notable one than Sullivan, ending his career as Superintendent of Brooklyn Psychiatric Hospital. Bellinger himself has some of the external marks that suggest homosexuality. He never married, and was apparently living with his mother in his mature years. That does not give anyone the warrant to label Bellinger homosexual either. Offense, of course, does sometimes make the best defense. But in any case, in Sullivan's view, pre-adolescent homosexual genital contact is of no consequence, except perhaps a beneficial one, preparing the way to later emerging heterosexual lust.

As an unmarried adult male, there were *sotto voce* comments about Sullivan's likely sexual life, and the presumption of his homosexuality. There is a report that, during his final years at Sheppard Pratt, he was labeled "Miss Sullivan" in the local gossip. That Sullivan established his all-male (both patients and staff) psychiatric ward at Sheppard Pratt undoubtedly turned a few heads and fueled such innuendo. Homosexuality was obviously on the agenda—at the very least *sub rosa*—in such an idiosyncratic project.

Sullivan made it his life's work to explicate the impending psychological issues in the preadolescent period for males, which he contended was psychodynamically and developmentally a homosexual period. His focus on that period may draw all kinds of suspicions, but it does not establish sexual facts about Sullivan's personal life.

Sullivan moved a 15-year-old vagrant boy, James Inscoe, into his home. James, a.k.a. Jimmie, was a street urchin whom Sullivan clearly loved. Sullivan treated the former street urchin as a son during the last two decades of his life. He legally adopted James, who assumed the surname "Sullivan," and designated him as the heir to his estate, what there was of it. The Sullivan-Inscoe relationship was clearly loving and close. But was it genitally consummated? Personally, I think that it probably was, but I do not have the warrant for declaring my assumption as fact. When the doors of our bedrooms are closed, no one can be sure what takes place there...or what does not.

As for Inscoe, two persons living together of any gender do not equate with two persons engaging in genital sex. Sullivan loved Inscoe, cared for him, and provided for him, but all manifestations of love do not lead ineluctably to genital sexual relations.

❖ ❖ ❖

Sullivan was a friend of the industrial designer and artist John Vassos. Vassos presented further data suggesting Sullivan identified himself as homosexual. At Sullivan's request, Vassos created a personal icon for the designation given him by his family as the "son of the west wind riding east to meet the dawn." This mythical construct was perhaps bestowed on Sullivan by his mother or his beloved Aunt Margaret during his childhood. The icon created by Vassos at Sullivan's direction—which can be seen in various books posthumously published under Sullivan's authorship—consists of two horses' heads, one facing up, and the other facing down... in other words, in the "69" position. According to Vassos, Sullivan specifically directed that the subtle lines in this icon delineate the numbers 6 and 9. This could certainly be taken as a message to the future regarding Sullivan's sexuality... *or, something else.* Innuendo, strong as it may be, does not constitute fact. The fact is, however, that "69", or *soixante-neuf* as the French say, is, while sexual, not by any means an *exclusively* homosexual allusion.

Vassos published *Phobia* in 1931 and dedicated it to "HSS." [35] Sullivan had done much of the work in writing the Introduction to the book, but he did not want his name to be used in print in that context. Sullivan invested considerable energy in seeing to it that the great mass of his writings were confined within the perimeters of academia and the clinic. And as research shows, he did a very good job of it.

The sexual proclivities of each of us are often clouded in one obfuscation or another, for obvious reasons. In this culture at least, and also in many others, but especially in this *American* culture, one can be brutally injured by public knowledge of one's out-of-the-mainstream sexual practices, whatever they are...most especially if they offend the common presumptive standards of the great unwashed middle class. That was particularly true in the American decades just prior to the Sexual Revolution of the 1960s. Nothing frightened the natives more powerfully than indications of *unconventional* sexual practices.

There was some gossip surrounding Sullivan, and confirmed by him, alleging that he almost married a woman, presumably his dear friend Clara Thompson. It is said that they spent an evening together and in the course of the evening vowed to marry. The next morning, each raced to the phone to call the other to void the engagement. Who got through first is not reported. According to R. Barton Evans III, [36] Sullivan himself acknowledged that such an incident did occur, though he did not link it with Thompson. That Thompson and Sullivan loved each other deeply over several decades is indisputable. Whether they contemplated marriage, or whether they engaged in genital sex, is not certain. But even if they did, that would be no proof that Sullivan was not to some extent homosexual, or bisexual.

Unless new documentation shows up, for now we must say that Sullivan's own personal sexual practices and/or so-called sexual orientation cannot be determined with reasonable certainty. He showed many of the typical marks of having been a practicing homosexual, but any public declaration that his sexual identity and personal practice was that of a practicing homosexual, or *gay*, is unsubstantiated. The scholars who have boldly declared Sullivan to have been *gay* have overreached. They cannot document what they claim. Furthermore, such a claim is also a tad anachronistic. In Sullivan's lifetime,

162

homosexuals were not publicly referred to as "gay," nor were they, for the most part in any sense, gay. They were generally outcasts among the middle class, and the great majority were severely abused socially.

Even when Sullivan calls homosexuality in mature years "a developmental mistake," we still cannot draw any significant conclusions from that about Sullivan's own personal life. He may simply have understood that his own life was "developmentally problematic." He indeed possessed that sort of basic self-awareness, self-assurance, and clinical objectivity.

The claim of a *gay Sullivan* is politically motivated, apparently designed to give the gay community one more distinguished subscriber to the subgroup. We should respect their wish for allies or distinguished fellow travelers, especially given all the public abuse they have received. However, we are all obliged to be accurate with regard to Sullivan's biography. If he did not personally own a homosexual identity in his lifetime—even apparently to his closest friends—I believe that outing him posthumously on circumstantial evidence alone is inappropriate and beyond that, offensive. The truth is that Sullivan may have lived a polymorphously perverse life with both genders. We simply do not know the details of what Sullivan's broad spectrum personal physical gratification of his *lust dynamism* might have been. And why that might actually matter very much to anyone now is also a bit of a mystery.

In Freud's view, everyone is in part homosexual; it is only a matter of degree. So, when someone declares Sullivan a homosexual, the proper response might be, "To what extent?" Or still more apt, "Aren't we all to some extent?" Sullivan may have been homosexual, heterosexual, bisexual, sexually inactive, or a running mixture of all the above and more. He kept his own counsel on the details of his own libidinal history, and he seems to have taken that data with him to the grave.

I consider it unacceptable to place the dead in a clear sexual classification unless they have gone on record for themselves or been conclusively outed by a third party as to the nature of their sexual practice. Genital pleasuring must not be assumed in any intimate relationship between persons of any configuration of genders. We cannot conclude, for example, that King David's grief over the death of his beloved Jonathan was the loss of a sexual partner:

"I grieve for you, Jonathan my brother;
dear and delightful you were to me;
your love for me was wonderful.
Surpassing that of a woman." [37]

Sullivan was extremely private. The only persons who seem to have significantly penetrated his privacy, and written about it, are Helen Swick Perry, Clara Thompson, Dorothy Blitsten, and David McKenzie Rioch, none of whom are known to have documented his sexual history or expressed the opinion that Sullivan was *homosexual*. Thompson, an intimate friend for almost all of Sullivan's professional life, was younger than Sullivan by only eighteen months, and she adored the man. Thompson delivered Sullivan's eulogy in 1948, which indicated where she stood in his galaxy. Helen Swick Perry, nineteen years younger than Sullivan, was his personal secretary for the last three years of his life. She had access to much of his personal data and correspondence, especially after his death, and she loved him as well. Dorothy Blitsten had a deep and loving relationship with Sullivan. She wrote about his theories but not his sexuality. David Rioch was part of the small circle of social friends and psychoanalytic colleagues of Sullivan and also wrote about him. He reveals nothing about Sullivan's sexuality. Among Sullivan's close friends—at least, those who are known to us—none has testified on the record, even posthumously, that he was homosexual.

The most likely account of Sullivan's sexual life is that he experienced precious little sexual pleasure of any sort. Even among friends he continued throughout his brief life to be the lonely, isolated farm boy, with no siblings and inadequate parents. It seems most likely that whatever sexual pleasure he found, whether homosexual or heterosexual, was very fleeting. The fact that he sheltered in his middle 30s a 14-year-old, troubled street urchin for lifelong companionship tells the basic story of Sullivan's emotional life. Margaret Rioch, who worked with Sullivan at Chestnut Lodge, is quoted saying that he was the loneliest functional person she ever knew. This view is also supported by Barton Evans. [38]

Finally, all the talk and writing that has been done about Sullivan's personal sexual life—and there has been a great amount of it—is interesting, but the bulk of it unsubstantiated and without real consequence. Sullivan's contribution to psychology, humanity, international relations, world peace, and the neglected among us, will not be diminished one iota by whatever data, if any, may finally emerge about his personal sexual practice. In the larger context of his astonishing life, the manner in which he may have been pleasured sexually is of very little consequence, except for prospective voyeurs.

IV

In 1945, Sullivan received two books by Wilhelm Reich in hopes of getting a review published in *Psychiatry*. Sullivan forwarded the books to Boisen for review. That was a very provocative move. Sullivan surely knew of Boisen's negative posture on any form of sexual liberation. There is no record of any conversation between them on the subject of Reich. However, evidence is plentiful that the two men saw Reich quite differently. Sullivan almost certainly found Reich a welcoming public voice, challenging the fear and fascination of sexual pleasure within the American middle class, and Boisen surely held an opposing view in *his* fear and fascination of the same. But there is no known record of any comment between Sullivan and Boisen on this subject...just as there is precious little information of what they discussed in general during their many meetings over 25 years.

Reich was evangelical about his own radical sexual liberalism. His public behavior, especially his countercultural sexual behavior and unabashed candor, made him something of a sexual wild man in the eyes of the public.

Reich was born in 1897, five years after Sullivan, and died in 1957, eight years after Sullivan. Reich began as something of a child prodigy within Freud's close inner circle. Freud trusted him enough with patients to assign him as deputy director of his outpatient clinic in the mid-1920s. But Reich soon became alienated due to his intense sexual liberationist views and behavior, and also because of his Marxist views. Thus, Freud dismissed him. Reich then traveled to Russia but was expelled by the Communists as well, again because of his preoccupation with sex. He was in Scandinavia at the onset of World War II and was fortunate enough to sail on the last boat out of Norway for New York, on August 19, 1939, just before the Nazi occupation. Helen Flanders Dunbar's husband, Theodore P. Wolfe, a Columbia University psychiatrist and an earlier student of Reich, assisted Reich's emigration into the United States, where he immediately found a teaching job at The New School in Manhattan. That did not last long either; Reich was dismissed from his teaching position in the summer of 1941. [39]

Reich was clearly a brilliant and creative person but with quite fluid boundaries and a wild and erratic lifestyle and reputation, with multiple wives and lovers. He also built a reputation for making claims that he could not fully support, the Orgone Box being the most spectacular. The Box, something similar to a small phone booth, was alleged to revitalize the libido of those who spent an appropriate amount of time inside it, preferably naked. On January 28, 1981, Arthur Dickerman, Professor at University of Oregon, was interviewed by the Food and Drug Administration (FDA) after he bought an Orgone Box, a.k.a. an "accumulator." He told the FDA that he did not believe it was effective in its stated purpose but that it kept his wife quietly occupied for four hours a day. [40]

Reich argued that orgone was a cosmic force related to the energy released in human orgasms. His Orgone Box was alleged to be an "orgone accumulator," a device for collecting orgone energy, which revitalized persons sitting in the box. Ultimately, Reich was charged by the FDA with selling his Boxes across state lines in violation of the law, convicted, and sent to federal prison. The FDA went a step further: they collected Reich's books, and on August 23, 1956, burned six tons of them at the Gansevoort Incinerator on West 26th Street in Manhattan. The bill for the cost of the burning was sent to Reich's Orgone Institute.

Whatever the merits—or lack thereof—of Reich's theories about orgone energy, the federal government was utterly reprehensible for burning Reich's scientific and published materials. It is incredible that in 1956— with the memory of Nazi book burnings fresh in everyone's mind—the U.S. government would conduct the largest book burning in American history.

Sullivan was never known to have made a public comment on Reich. Nor is there a known record of any conversation about Reich between Boisen and Sullivan. However, Boisen reviewed the two books as assigned for *Psychiatry, and* quite professionally. While he criticized Reich, he did so in a thoughtful and scholarly manner. He also contended that Reich differed from "Malinowski's balanced conclusions," undoubtedly unaware of the friendly Malinowski-Reich correspondence taking place. But he also applauded Reich for promoting lasting sexual relationships and for advocating a replacement of authoritarian and legalistic family structure with inner responsibility. Boisen's final sentence, though not positive, was judicious: "The question may be raised whether his [Reich's] philosophy of life may not all too readily lend itself to the undergirding of the inevitable postwar moral let-down." [41] Under the watchful eye of Sullivan, Boisen was more measured in his judgments about sexuality than when he was when presenting his views to fellow pastors.

When I was engaged in my own clinical pastoral training in the mid-1960s, I never witnessed any discussion of Reich in training seminars. However, I did note that Reich's books appeared on the office book shelves of various clinical pastoral supervisors whom I knew and with whom I worked. One of them was the late Winton Gable, who became a close friend of mine and who began his career as chaplain at Terrill State in Texas in 1957. He had followed Walter Bell, who was a Council for Clinical Training and later Association for Clinical Pastoral Education supervisor and a Reichian therapist himself. Gable related to me that Bell attended meetings of the Council with an Orgone Box strapped to the roof of his automobile. I recall Gable referring to certain psychiatric patient treatments at Terrill State Hospital under Bell in which patients of both sexes would be asked to strip down to their underwear for therapy sessions in the Reichian mode. I recall also that Winton was hesitant to follow Bell in his full blown Reichian process. But he was certainly intrigued by the Reichian approach. I have a wistful fantasy of calling Walter Bell back from the grave for a tour of American attitudes toward sexuality. My fantasy is that he would say that he's glad he's gone.

In the late 1950s, Reich was convicted of sending his Orgone Box across state lines in violation of federal law and sentenced to two years in federal prison. Reich was first sent to Danbury Federal Prison on March 19, 1957, not quite 60 years old. He was later transferred to Lewisburg Federal Penitentiary. He was due to be released November 10, 1957. His last letter to his son was written on October 22. Reich was found dead in bed, fully clothed, on November 3, seven days prior to his scheduled release. Heart failure was the stated cause of death.

There is no clear consensus on Reich, either by presumed experts in the field or the broader public. He is now generally viewed either as a madman—a psychopath—or a greatly misunderstood progressive, scientific, and humanistic genius. He may well have been a little bit of each.

1. Sullivan, Harry Stack, ed. Helen Swick Perry, with an Introduction by Otto Allen Will. (1954). *The Psychiatric Interview.* New York: W. W. Norton & Company, p. 169.

2. Sullivan, *The Fusion of Psychiatry and Social Science, op. cit.,* p. 72.

3. Sullivan, Harry Stack. (1947). *Conceptions of Modern Psychiatry.* Washington, D.C.: The William Alanson White Foundation, p. 63. (Hereafter, CMP.)

4. Lawrence, Raymond J. (1989). *The Poisoning of Eros, Sexual Values in Conflict.* New York: Augustine Moore Press, pp. 66–195.

5. Sullivan, Harry Stack. (1953). *The Interpersonal Theory of Psychiatry.* New York: W. W. Norton & Company Inc., New York, pp. 293–296. (Hereafter, ITP.)

6. Ibid.

7. Ibid., p. 271.

8. Ibid., pp. 294–5.

9. Sullivan, Harry Stack. (1962). *Schizophrenia As a Human Process.* New York: W. W. Norton & Company, Inc., p. 104. (Hereafter, SHP.)

10. ITP, p 275, 372.

11. Ibid., p. 272.

12. Ibid., pp. 278–9.

13. Ibid.

14. Ibid., p.287

15. Joshua 2:9-23; p. 242, *The New English Bible (NEB) The Old Testament; and Hebrews* 11:31, *NEB, The New Testament,* p. 289.

16. ITP, pp. 282–296, passim.

17. Sullivan, Harry Stack; Introduction by Helen Swick Perry. (1965). *Personal Psychopathology*. Washington, D.C.: The William Alanson White Foundation, p. 324. (Hereafter, PP.)

18. Ibid., p. 195.

19. Robert G. Kvarnes. (1976). *A Harry Stack Sullivan Case Seminar*. New York: W. W. Norton and Company Inc., p. 216–217.

20. ITP, p. 289.

21. Sullivan, CMP, p. 60.

22. Ibid., p. 61.

23. ITP, p. 296.

24. Sullivan, *Conceptions of Modern Psychiatry, op. cit.*, p. 58. /EVANS 202

25. Sullivan, SHP, 203,212

26. Sullivan, CMP, 211 [ITP, 294].

27. Hunter, Mic, ed, The Sexually Abused Male: Prevalence, Impact, and Treatment, Lexington, MA: Lexington Books, 1990.

28. TPI, 237–9

29. Ibid.

30. ITP, 246

31. Cornett, Carlton, (2017), *Being with Patients, An Introduction to the Psychotherapy of Harry Stack Sullivan, M.D., and Otto Allen Will, Jr., M.D.* Kingston Springs, TN: Westview, p. 40.

32. Kvarnes, *op. cit.*, pp. 24–26

33. Perry, p. 313.

34. Ibid., 204, 313.

35. Vassos, John, *Phobia*, Covici Friede Publishers, NY, 1931.

36. Evans, *op. cit.*, p. 37.

37. *The New English Bible*, Oxford University Press, 1970, p. 340.

38. Personal communication.

39. Thornton, Edward E., (1970) *Professional Education for Ministry: A History of Clinical Pastoral Education*, Nashville: Abingdon Press, p. 92.

40. Interview of Dickerman by the FDA, 28 January, 1981, posted on Wikipedia.

41. *Psychiatry*, 1945, 8:4.

CHAPTER 9

Sullivan and Dorothy Rubovits Blitsten

༄

I n 1932, the psychoanalyst N. Lionel Blitzsten invited Sullivan to Chicago for consultative reasons not specifically registered. Very likely it was assistance in building an alliance with him subsequent to the arrival of Franz Alexander in Chicago in 1930. Blitzsten was the first psychoanalyst in Chicago, and in fact the first west of New York City, having begun practice there in the early 1920s. All three men were in their late 30s, within a year or two of each other in age. Thus, Alexander became the second Chicago-based psychoanalyst. [1]

Alexander was a Hungarian who had been analyzed by Otto Rank in Vienna. Freud had engaged him to analyze his own son Oliver; a public demonstration of Freud's confidence in Alexander. Thus, Alexander already had something of a reputation in the field when Robert Hutchins, then the President of the University of Chicago, invited him to become Visiting Professor of Psychiatry. More to the point, Alexander had been Lionel Blitzsten's own analyst in Berlin several years previously. Blitzsten is said to have cut the analysis short due to his wife's illness. Pauline Wolf Blitzsten, his first wife, died in January, 1928. [2]

Alexander created the Chicago Psychiatric Institute in 1932, a move undoubtedly felt by Blitzsten to be something of a threat to his status as the pioneer psychoanalyst in Chicago. Douglas W. Orr, a eulogist who contributed to the Blitzsten Memorial Book, reported that Blitzsten had been estranged from the Chicago Institute but did not know why. Both Alexander and Blitzsten were simultaneously associated with the University of Chicago in some fashion. However, according to Helen Swick Perry, Alexander left his position at the University after only one year, undoubtedly to direct his own Chicago Institute of Psychoanalysis. One year after Alexander's beginning with the University would have been the fall of 1931. [3]

In 1932, Blitzsten invited Harry Stack Sullivan to visit him; the agenda was not recorded. Blitzsten had recently married his former student and analysand, Dorothy Rubovits, 14 years his junior. It is suggested that the marriage became rocky quite early on, and at some point the couple divorced. In March 1942, Lionel printed new stationery dropping the "z" in his name. His friends teased him about castrating himself. He continued to use both spellings for the remaining decade of his life. Subsequent to the divorce, Dorothy kept her married name, but also without the "z." She also moved to New York City in 1945, probably already divorced. [4]

When Sullivan arrived in Chicago, Dorothy met him at the train station. As Dorothy told it, after Sullivan's arrival and an extended awkwardness in the car—typical of Sullivan—he finally asked her if she might be kin to one of his medical school professors two decades earlier at the Chicago College of Medicine and Surgery, with the name Rubovits. She answered yes, that the professor was her father, William H. Rubovits. (Dorothy, born in 1907, must have been about six years old when Sullivan attended her father's classes.)

Hearing this, Sullivan relaxed. Her father had been one of only two instructors, according to Sullivan, whom the students had respected. Sullivan shared with Dorothy that he himself often slept in class, as he was living hand-to-mouth and usually worked nights. Rubovits taught obstetrics, a subject of little interest to Sullivan. In one class, as Sullivan recounted it, Rubovits asked a question that no one in the class could answer. After 20 years, Sullivan could not remember the exact question, but he recalled the answer that he blurted out after being roused from sleep by a classmate: "the psychosis of pregnancy." Sullivan was correct, and Rubovits congratulated him for his astuteness. Sullivan believed that Rubovits had passed him on the basis of that one answer. [5]

In succeeding years, Sullivan visited the Blitzstens often. With his frequent travels, Chicago was usually the place to change trains, and sometimes planes, and that gave Sullivan many opportunities to visit them. In the course of the next 18 years, Sullivan developed very significant but dissimilar personal relationships with each of them. He was also asked by Lionel to provide him further psychoanalysis, and he did so. Leonard Blitzsten seems to have shared in common with Sullivan a certain audacity and a practice of testing boundaries in his work with students and trainees. He informally labeled one of his academic courses on human development, "From Infantility to Adultery." His students and trainees referred to his *blitzing,* and claimed to have been *blitzkrieged.* His former trainees seemed to have referred to themselves as *S.O.B.s,* or *Sons of Blitzsten.* Thus, it is no wonder that he bonded with Sullivan. [6]

Through the years, Sullivan also clearly developed quite an intimate personal relationship with Dorothy and an obvious fondness for her, which she reciprocated. Reading Sullivan's letters to Dorothy, a husband prone to jealousy might have concluded that the two were sexually involved; and perhaps they were. Sullivan usually, but not always, wrote the couple separately, adding greetings to "the other" in his final salutation. On each of Dorothy's birthdays, she received a greeting from Sullivan signed with "love." She wrote that it was often said that Sullivan "did not get along with women…but nothing was further from the truth," she countered. [7]

At some point, probably in the early 1940s, the Blitzstens presumably divorced. While a divorce date itself does not seem easily obtainable, the separation was. Dorothy moved alone to New York City in 1945. The apparent rationale for their separation was that their sexual attraction for each other had diminished or disappeared on one side or the other, or both. Sullivan, in a very personal letter, attempted strongly to dissuade them from divorcing, pointing out that such radical acts usually bring more pain than pleasure.

In a letter specifically addressed to Dorothy on November 7, 1940, Sullivan, in his all-too-typical and clumsy English, wrote:

"In the limited field of sexual intimacy, the course had been away from such intimacies and there is no sufficient determining influence to change its direction. In many other fields of behavior, the course seems to be quite satisfactory. A perfectionist might be willing to forego everything, if there was any imperfection. A person lost in psychoanalytic thinking might feel that the absence of lustful rapport indicated that everything was wrong. Both these attitudes seem to me tedious in the extreme…It seems to me that you give each other a good deal that is valuable and that it is deplorable that there are verbal attacks and appeals to the 'will' and 'deciding' for the alteration of this relationship to something other than it now is." [8]

Sullivan's letter has some of the timbre of an autopsy. Clearly, he sided with Dorothy emotionally, but was also on the side of the Blitzstens remaining married. His advice to her was consistent with his view that lust and sexual congress in a marital relationship typically wane as the years pass, and were not, in any case, essential to marital love and intimacy; the same perspective which Sullivan consistently promoted, and one to which most of the non-Christian world cultures subscribe. Subsequently, Sullivan continued to stay in contact with both of the Blitzstens, but more closely with Dorothy. He typically referred to Lionel in letters to Dorothy, in words such as, "Much love to you and a supplemental measure of love for Lionel to be delivered when you see him." [9]

Whether there had been a sexual liaison or not, we likely will never know, and surely it matters not. Dorothy was clearly enamored of Sullivan;

there seems no doubt but that she would have made herself sexually available to him if requested. And he clearly loved her. Their separate correspondence over the years was more prolific and far more endearing than the correspondence between Lionel and Sullivan. That, of course, would be expected since Sullivan was Lionel's analyst.

After Sullivan's death, Dorothy described him as a slight, physically slim man who commanded attention when he spoke. His thinking, she said, was unusual, illuminating, and witty. She reported that he was a heavy smoker, something that does not seem to appear in other records. (Of course, in that era smoking was almost universal.) There was an austerity about him, in her view. He could be moody and withdrawn. But no one, she said, was more responsive to the needs of others. She added that he was something of a firebrand. She is clearly describing her own personal experience of Sullivan.

Dorothy added that Sullivan had "a strange non-Protestant attitude toward money." Thrift saving and capital accumulation were not part of his lifestyle. Did she think that Sullivan was Protestant? Perhaps. "A little money was a dangerous goad to Sullivan," she wrote, which was allegedly supported by Sullivan himself with the comment, "like the child that I am regarding money." [10] Sullivan shared with Dorothy the fact that the Internal Revenue Service constantly harassed him. [11] Lionel himself was said to have become a source of funds for Sullivan from time to time as were many of his other friends. Dorothy also painted a dark picture of Sullivan's relationship with Harold D. Lasswell, a psychiatrist and political scientist and long-standing friend and colleague of Sullivan's, whom he later charged with "agile opportunism, and misappropriating funds." Dorothy thought Sullivan unfair to Lasswell. She may well have been right. [12]

Dorothy described Sullivan's posture as "habitually perplexed and continually inquiring" and never "dogmatic except in opposing dogma." He was "a towering and compelling influence" and his "criticisms of other views were often devastating." She added that Sullivan especially loved Ross Chapman, his administrator at Sheppard Pratt. [13]

Dorothy also described in detail the propensity of the various psychiatric authorities to fight with each other, and with venom. And Sullivan was always willing to enter a fight amongst them. He was particularly caustic with towards Gregory Zilboorg and Franz Alexander. About the former, Sullivan himself reported that he told Zilboorg that he "was intellectually dishonest." And after Sullivan presented a paper at a psychoanalytic meeting in Chicago, to which Franz Alexander had attended, and raised objections, Sullivan recorded the following exchange: "Alexander's bulk had prevented him from reaching me instantly (after the lecture)…but (eventually) he assured me that I was mistaken." He added that there was talk among some that "the bovine Alexander should replace Abraham Brill" as the putative "American Freud." [14]

It can be assumed that Sullivan in all events came to the defense of his protégé, and competitor of Alexander, Lionel Blitzsten.

Dorothy once asked Sullivan what he would do first if he had authority to do anything he wished in the field of psychiatry. He replied that he would call a moratorium on all psychotherapeutic treatments and activities, and would free psychiatrists to train lay people full time as "participant observers," which is to say, "lay psychotherapists." [15] Sullivan consistently favored lay psychotherapists in preference to professionals. He redefined the psychotherapeutic role as that of "participant observer." This role embraced lay persons and clergy as well psychiatrists. This position surely accounts in part for the overwhelming disdain he received from so many of his psychiatric colleagues. Sullivan's praise of Anton Boisen as a psychotherapist in gatherings of psychotherapists would likely have stirred up similar boundary anxiety among psychiatrists. And at Sheppard Pratt he created an entire therapeutic staff out of non-psychiatrists, consisting even of low-level orderlies, a therapeutic staff that achieved an astonishing 80 to 86% cure rate.

A mutual friend of Dorothy's once said, "I never left Sullivan without feeling that a cubit had been added to my self-esteem." Sullivan's consistent *modus operandi* was to empower the weak—and to disempower the strong. [16]

In the middle 1930s Dorothy authored a pamphlet on her own initiative on the subject of psychoanalysis and from her own perspective. Sullivan persuaded her to read it to a dinner party group consisting of William V. (Billy) Silverberg and Earnest E. Hadley, each psychiatrists and longstanding friends and colleagues of his. It is not stated whether Lionel was present. Sullivan liked the pamphlet and suggested it be published. He decided to edit the piece for her in getting it ready for publication. Dorothy later wrote that she wished he had not. It was a simple document and entirely her own. But that imposition on the part of Sullivan did not disqualify Sullivan from her epithet describing him as "a perfect friend in need." [17]

After Dorothy moved to New York City, she and Sullivan had a standing date for lunch on the first Monday after the last Sunday of the month. Sometimes she saw him for dinner instead. Sullivan pressed her to get an advanced degree. "I never wanted to see another classroom," she said, "but he persuaded me to enroll at Columbia for a Ph.D. in *Sociology*." She seems to have matriculated in 1945.

Dorothy was the last person to see Sullivan alive on American soil. His evening flight to Europe, in early January 1949, was delayed until the next morning, and he invited her to meet him for dinner. She noted that he seemed more exhausted than usual. His flight took off the next morning. She never saw him again; he died in Paris two weeks later. Sullivan used to say, "If I die one day under a hundred, I'll die enraged." He missed making it to one hundred by more than four decades. [18]

❖ ❖ ❖

Dorothy herself earned a Ph.D. in Sociology at Columbia in tandem with her psychoanalytic training and without an M.D. She published a monograph in 1953 entitled *The Social Theories of Harry Stack Sullivan.* [19] It was the same year that Perry and her editorial team published the first collection of Sullivan's papers, *The Interpersonal Theory of Psychiatry.* Blitsten's work is one of the most astute, and along with Patrick Mullahy, among the earliest of any works professing to elucidate the often-impenetrable theory and practice of Sullivan, of which there are of course only a very few. It is not an exaggeration to say that Dorothy Blitsten became an authentic Sullivanian. She had also published *Psychoanalysis Explained* in 1936, the pamphlet Sullivan encouraged her to write and edited for her. [20]

Blitsten illuminated in particular the sense in which Sullivan linked psychiatry and psychoanalysis with sociology. The link was strong. Blitsten cites Georg Simmel for his definition: "Sociology…is the study of the forms of socialization: it is assigned to investigate all forms of socialization, not merely those which have become objectified in social institutions." [21] Simmel's definition of sociology is congruent with Sullivan's revision of psychiatry as that of an examination of relationships.

In certain relatively private contexts late in life, Sullivan referred to himself as a social scientist with a specialty in psychiatry. This posture was congruent with his thesis that interpersonal relationships are the non-negotiable element in being human, and that they are the entirety of what we are as persons. This thesis is contained in the bright light Sullivan placed on the pre-adolescent phase of human development as the phase of life during which the individual becomes significantly relational beyond the nexus of the family of origin. Sullivan was *the* psychoanalyst of pre-adolescence in the same way that Freud was the psychoanalyst of the Oedipal drama. That is not to suggest that this is all the two men knew, but that their focus repeatedly returned to those particular points of transition in life, or developmental dramas.

Many authorities seem to use such distinctions as a way of elevating one form of psychiatry and diminishing the other. But such polarization is counterproductive. Both Freud and Sullivan possessed their own unique kind of genius, each with his own perspective and special emphases. Using one to diminish the other, as seems to be a popular stance, is counterproductive, even destructive. Psychiatrists, or psychotherapists of any discipline, are like the proverbial blind examining the elephant. They draw their conclusions—sometimes rigid ones—based on the part of the elephant they are able to feel and in unawareness of the parts of the elephant that they cannot touch. Perhaps none are wrong. But all knowledge is limited, hemmed in by personal experience or lack thereof.

Sullivan moved psychiatry out of the narrow focus of mental illness where modern culture had placed it. In general, in the current culture, one would presume that anyone going to see a psychiatrist is doing so only if suspected of being mentally troubled or ill. For Sullivan, as well as for Freud, such assumptions were grossly misleading. Of course, the mentally disturbed are typically referred to psychiatrists, but in Sullivan's and Freud's constructs, good psychiatry should be accessible to everyone as a continuing resource for living effectively in the world of relationships. However, an economic problem emerges here, namely that psychiatry, having been held captive by the medical profession, is therefore available only to the financially resourceful. That conundrum may very well illuminate both Sullivan's investment in lay psychotherapy and his significant and positive relationship with Anton Boisen. Boisen, as a teacher of pastors, brought psychotherapy into the religious communities at a price that working people could afford. Indeed, Boisen enlarged that vision in a significant way through his clinical pastoral training movement. Boisen was shaping religious professionals into non-medical psychotherapists with the backing of Sullivan and the theoretical backing of Freud. Unfortunately, since Boisen's death, the clinical pastoral training movement that Boisen almost singlehandedly created has undertaken a massive and regressive retreat, largely abandoning the psychotherapeutic role. Pastors for the most part do not read Boisen anymore, or for that matter Sullivan, or Freud. Boisen's clinical training movement has mostly devolved into a prayer and spirituality movement, completely subverting the psychoanalytic dimensions of training that were central to the movement he created.

Medicine as a science focuses on diseases located in particular physical aspects of organisms. Thus, psychiatry has similarly been widely perceived as a study of a mental illness *in* particular persons. Brain disease obviously does occur; therefore, it is possible that a person might be afflicted with an invasive organism, a developmental aberration, or a chemical intrusion that affects mental status. Addressing the intrusion medically in that case is appropriate. However, Sullivan's argument was that the bulk of psychiatric disturbance is relational, not organic, and is formed out of troubled relationships with other persons.

Sullivan thus described his work in his select psychiatric ward at Sheppard; work which made him famous as "a school for personality growth" rather than a custodial form of care for personality failures or medical treatment for schizophrenia. [22]

Dorothy Blitsten wrote that Sullivan rejected Freud's libidinal theory of personality development. [23] That judgment is probably too categorical and too harsh. It appears rather that Sullivan significantly expanded Freud's libidinal theory in favor of a broader view of human psychological suffering. Sullivan, in his own words, replaced Freud's oral, anal, and phallic foci of sexual pleasure with oral, retinal, auditory, general tactical, vestibular kinesthetic, *genital,* and *anal* foci. The italics, said Sullivan, are to signify those foci which vary from person to person because of cultural influences. [22] Sullivan was, in contrast to Freud, continually turning down the volume on sex, or perhaps we should say, adding additional foci, which in effect gave less attention to genital pleasure as such. Or, perhaps we should not say *less attention* and rather say *less time on the clock.*

Freud was productive in *fin de siècle* Europe and all its obsession with and repression of sexuality, while Sullivan was a product of a somewhat different country and different era. This is not the context for parsing the differences between the generations and cultures, even if we were able, but it is important to understand that each person is a product of a certain time and culture and therefore has a right to be different without being wrong. Certainly, it would be an error to claim that Sullivan was focused on relationship and Freud was not, or less so. The two men worked from different frames and in different cultural constructs. Sullivan was at once more focused on sex than Freud, as in his attention to the inexorability of lust, and less so than Freud, as in his unequivocally placing mutually caring human relationships at the pinnacle of human values.

Sullivan added that the oral zone is involved in such varied functions that it is perhaps the central trunk for the evolution of the self. The genital zone is so conditioned by the prejudices and biases of parents that it is apt to be permanently impaired in its biological function, if not for all forms of interpersonal activity. [23] Sullivan also rejected the necessity of postulating a kind of pseudo-anthropology for man to explain the origins of his behavior, such as Jung's archetypes or Freud's primal Oedipal situation. [24]

As Sullivan put it, the first need of the human being is the satisfaction of food and water, and the second is security. One issue that Sullivan spoke of incessantly is *security operations.* It is a distinctly Sullivanian concept. He invented it and gave it its meaning: that the creation and maintenance of a kind of secure self-respect in the context of an often-hostile world was not negotiable. Sullivan avoided at all cost leaving a patient or friend feeling insecure on parting. A feeling of safety in the esteem of others was the principal way Sullivan defined security operations. Anxiety, said Sullivan, can never be deferred. It seems clear that he spoke largely out of his own experience. As Sullivan himself put it, sudden, severe anxiety probably is never much more educative than a severe blow to the head. [25]

Sullivan emphasized the communal nature of human experience. For Sullivan, there exists no durable, unique, individual personality aside from what is shaped through relationships. Each person's pattern of interpersonal relationships is itself unique and creates a relatively enduring pattern of interpersonal relationships. But that uniqueness has no independent or intrinsic standing. Sullivan supported Aristotle's axiom, "give me the child… and I will show you the man," declaring the fact of both the plasticity of human personality and the possibility of shaping a personality, particularly in the early years. He added, "much more is going on in the young child than simply nursing and sphincter control." [26]

Sullivan was not alone in creating his own lingo, and one of his more commonly employed self-made categories was *parataxic distortion*. As many have said, it is a horrendous term, though etymologically it is indeed more accurate than *transference*, which it was meant to supplant. Its meaning is more or less the same as Freud's transference; that is, the distortion in our perception of others driven by our own experiences, fantasies, and wishes. After Sullivan's death the term seems also to have gone to its grave with him. The roots of such distortion reside in the unconscious, another term of Freud's that Sullivan hesitated to use very often. For those who are not Ph.D. psychiatrists, like me, the best illustration of transference, and *parataxic* distortion, is the process of falling in love. The object of one's affection will turn out to be at least a little bit different from one's original image, an image created by the viewer, and more often than not a hell of a lot different, much to the ultimate grief of many of those countless millions of persons who fall in love every day. [27]

Sullivan contended that the purely communicative aspect of speech has been exaggerated. [28] This claim is supported by the fact of authentic communication between infants and mothers, or fathers; that is, communication that transcends speech...what Sullivan calls "prototaxic symbol activity," by which he means pre-language communication, the communication of infants who do not use words at all. (Sullivan could just as well have labeled this "non-verbal communication.") This *prototaxic symbol activity* would explain how subhuman animals, as well as prehistoric human beings, might have communicated prior to the development of speech and language. I personally have often wondered how prehistoric humans may have communicated prior to the development of language, and Sullivan is enlightening on that matter, suggesting that prehistoric humans may have communicated even *more* effectively prior to the development of language. Sullivan's contention is that such non-speech communication continues into the present, as with infants, the autistic, and schizophrenics as well, and that such communication trumps verbal communication.

Sullivan himself demonstrated this ability to communicate with schizophrenics by creating a psychiatric ward consisting solely of schizophrenics, achieving stunning results. The Yale sociologist Edward Sapir, who worked closely with Sullivan in the 1930s, contended that language is what it is, not because of the admirable expressive power of words but in spite of them. If one attends closely to the language of modern telecommunication, one gets the sense that language is actually used deliberately to obfuscate. Modern advertising is surely an example of that, and the linguistic methods of say, Donald Trump, or other public speakers who repeatedly say one thing while intending to communicate something quite different. As Sullivan says, "the purely communicative aspect of speech has been exaggerated." [29] The modern channels of communication—the mass media—have been disappointing as pertains to their capacity for authentic communication. One thinks of Adolf Hitler, whose actual words were often quite different from what he covertly attempted to communicate; something along the lines of, "all the people whom you hate will soon perish at my hands." And at this, many rejoiced, because they actually heard what he was saying, and he was saying what they wanted to hear, which was not revealed explicitly in a literal reading of his words.

Sullivan pointed out that the postulate of the unconscious is designed to provide a container or repository for all the discontinuity of conscious life. Sullivan did not actually dismiss the usefulness of the metaphor of the unconscious, but he did take a little poke at it in his Sullivanian manner. Referring specifically to the unconscious, he said "…that's bully, but don't be tempted to tell the world all about the unconscious, because someone is almost certain to ask you how you found out." In other words, if it is indeed unconscious, how is it that you can talk about it? Sullivan accepted the postulate of the unconscious but scoffed at those who talked about it as if they had it in their pocket. Sullivan preferred the label "selective inattention" rather than the premise of the unconscious, but substantively, they amount to the same thing for him. He contended that the concept of the unconscious is "very useful for theory, but not phenomenologically describable." [30]

Sullivan's approach to the treatment of psychotics, and in fact all patients, was to strengthen what he referred to as "the self-system." By self-system, Sullivan meant the confident sense of self held together by a variety of thoughts and experiences in relation to other persons. The collapse of a self-system is, according to Sullivan, what leads to progressive anxiety and ultimately psychosis. In his treatment of patients Sullivan constantly attended to such potential regression and the danger of a personality collapse. When he concluded that a particular patient needed to be confronted on a matter, he would regularly confront that person only near the beginning of a session so that he would have time remaining in the session to assist the patient in restoring his sense of self, his self-system.

The collapse of a self-system is marked by embarrassment, shame, humiliation, or a derogation of the self. It is manifest most often in selective inattention. In this state, one simply misses all sorts of things, which may cause embarrassment, or in many instances, of great profit not to notice. "It is the means by which you stay as you are in spite of the efforts of worthy psychiatrists, clergymen, and others to help you mend your ways. The metaphors of security operations and self-systems fit together like hand and glove. [31]

Sullivan defined psychiatry as the science of living under the conditions that prevail in a given social order. Therefore, psychiatry, in Sullivan's view, is a social science and relevant to more than simply mental illness. Sullivan's formulation is more than a classificatory scheme. The development of personality traits he considered as evidence of an organic integration process that includes the use of symbols as tools. The function of anxiety and the maintenance of self-systems disclose how people are attached to the societies in which they live. Sullivan was one of the first among psychiatrists—if not *the* first—to insist that the findings of sociologists and anthropologists made it necessary for psychiatrists to expand their field of observation and reformulate their concepts.

Sullivan labeled his communication with patients as participant-observation. And it may well be that he paid more attention to what he saw than to what he heard. He had little patience with anything he could not observe. As Sullivan put it, "Verbal performance is only tenuously related to reliable communication." Speech is a ticklish source of scientific data. Words cannot be conceived as having inherent "objective" meaning. "Parataxic" ("transferential" in Freudian language) elements in experience and the autistic fringes of language are seldom if ever missing from human behavior, according to Sullivan. [32]

Dorothy Blitsten became a preeminent Sullivan exegete in that first generation subsequent to Sullivan's death, along with David McKenzie Rioch, Helen Swick Perry, and some lesser-knowns. The fact that Sullivan earlier was a student of Blitsten's father and later her husband's consultant and psychoanalyst was quite a remarkable concatenation of relationships, bordering on the incestuous, and typical of Sullivan.

---

1. Note: the spelling of the name Blitzsten is inconsistent. The "z" is sometimes dropped, and later it was dropped entirely by Dorothy.

2. *The Blitzsten Memorial Book entitled N. Lionel Blitzs, M.D., Psychoanalist, Teacher, Friend, 1893–1952*, was a small, privately circulated book, published for the Lionel Blitzsten Memorial, Inc., by the International Universities Press, Inc., for private distribution only, 1961. Lionel Blitzsten had died in 1952.

3. Perry, Helen Swick. (1982). *Psychiatrist of America: The Life of Harry Stack Sullivan*. Cambridge, MA: The Belknap Press of Harvard University, p. 279.

4. Perry. *op. cit.*, p. 160.

5. "Lionel Blitzsten, The Teacher", by Douglass W. Orr, pp. 21–70, in the Blitzsten Memorial Book, *op. cit.*

6. Quinter, Janice, ed. (1987). *Dorothy R. Blitsten Memoir*. New York: The Oskar Diethelm Library, DeWitt Wallace Institute for the History of Psychiatry, Weill Cornell Medical College, October, p. 131.

7. Perry, *op. cit.*, p. 336.

8. Quinter, *op. cit.*, p. 147.

9. Harry Stack Sullivan: The Man and His Part in a Professional Revolution, Dorothy R. Blitsten, (unpublished) held in the Oscar Diethelm Collection, Dewitt Wallace Institute for the History of Psychiatry, Weill Cornell Medical College, p. 147

10. Ibid., pp. 27–8, 38.

11. Ibid., p. 134.

12. Blitsten, *A Memoir.* (unpublished) *op. cit.*, p. 29. Dorothy thought Sullivan was implacably hostile toward Lasswell, and that he was not guilty of the charges Sullivan leveled against him.

13. Blitsten, *Harry Stack Sullivan: Memoir,* pp. 51–52; also, Perry, *op. cit.,* pp. 286–288.

14. Ibid., p. 109.

15. Ibid., p. 109.

16. Ibid., p. 151.

17. Blitsten, *Harry Stack Sullivan Memoir*, p. 51–52

18. Blitzsten, Dorothy. (1953). *The Social Theories of Harry Stack Sullivan* New York: The William Frederick Press. (Hereafter," STHSS.")

19. Blitsten, Dorothy R. *Psychoanalysis Explained.* With an Introduction by A.A. Brill, M.D., Coward McConn Inc., New York, 1936. (Note the spelling of Blitzsten here.)

20. STHSS.

21. STHSS, p. 22. Originally "Socio-Psychiatric Research", in *Am. J. of Psychiatry*, pp. 982–985

22. Ibid., p. 17.

23. Ibid., p. 36.

24. Ibid., pp. 42; 83.

25. Ibid., p. 70.

26. Ibid., p. 84.

27. Citing Sapir, "Language," Encyclopedia of Social Sciences, p. 159.

28. Blitsten, STHSS, *op. cit.,* p. 124.

29. Ibid., pp. 145–8.

30. Ibid., pp. 144ff.

31. Ibid., pp. 157–163.

CHAPTER 10

The Nexus of Sullivan, Thompson, and Ferenczi

ॐ

Sullivan met Clara Thompson in April 1923, shortly after he arrived at Sheppard Pratt. He went to hear her present her very first scientific paper to a psychoanalytic meeting. The paper was entitled "Suicide and Psychosis." She was sickly at the time, with a temperature of 105, and had typhoid fever, unknowingly. Sullivan's immediate thought was, "My God, that woman is schizophrenic—I must know her!" Since Sullivan had a special affinity for schizophrenics, being one himself, he approached her and they were soon friends. Thompson wrote that Sullivan was disappointed to find out later that she wasn't schizophrenic. Thompson added parenthetically in her account: "I won't say that I wasn't schizophrenic!" Nevertheless, the relationship began and morphed into arguably Sullivan's most important friendship of his professional life. [1]

Later, in 1926, Sandor Ferenczi, on an American speaking tour, spoke in both Baltimore and New York City. Sullivan heard several of his lectures and was impressed. Ferenczi was 20 years older than Sullivan with substantially more years of experience. At that time, he was also Freud's designated "psychoanalytic heir," having replaced Carl Jung who was dethroned just prior to the First World War. When Freud reached age 50, he became very attentive to the question of whom he would name as his intellectual successor. He was quite happy to find Jung, partly because Jung was a Protestant of sorts, and at least not Jewish; that psychoanalysis was coming to be seen as "a Jewish science" was worrisome to Freud. But as the Great War approached, Jung and Freud also fell into interpersonal warfare, and Freud removed him from his appointed place of honor. The appointment of Jung was never going to last in any case; while Hitler was in the process of ridding Germany of its Jews, he was also ridding it of most of its psychoanalysts, most of whom were Jewish.

Jung wrote that "the factual and widely known difference between German and Jewish psychiatry should no longer be blurred." [2] To fill in for the absence of Jewish psychoanalytic leadership, Jung joined a relative of Hermann Goering's to become Co-President of the German Psychoanalytic Association. After 1939, he finally turned critical of Hitler, from the safety of Switzerland.

After Jung and Freud parted ways, Sandor Ferenczi became Freud's next successor designee. Ferenczi lasted until 1930, when he, too, was dismissed by Freud from that informal but honorary position. Freud was ultimately vexed by Ferenczi's fluid physical boundaries in his work with patients. He was not concerned from an ethical perspective, but rather from a public relations one. After hearing Ferenczi speaking on his U.S. tour in 1926, Sullivan proposed in a letter to William Alanson White that he invite Ferenczi to St. Elizabeths for a speaking engagement. It only took two days for White to decline the proposal in writing. It must be assumed that White noted Ferenczi's radicalism, and radicalism was not White's style. He had had enough headaches of that kind already in his support of Sullivan.

But Sullivan did not give up. He prevailed upon his friend Clara Thompson to go to Budapest in the summer of 1928, get psychoanalyzed by Ferenczi, and bring back Ferenczi's philosophy and psychoanalytic approach by psychoanalyzing Sullivan in the same manner. It seemed to have been a quite unrealistic expectation, but she complied, accompanied on her first of several trips by Erich Fromm and Karen Horney. Thompson took a liking to Ferenczi and Budapest. She repeated the trip in 1929, and in 1931, returned later to stay "as long as it took." She returned home some months after Ferenczi died in May 1933. Some of her American patients actually traveled to Budapest to continue treatment with her. While in Budapest, Thompson also took a handsome, spirited American businessman about her age as a lover, which made her Budapest stay all the more pleasurable. During at least some of her time with Ferenczi, she saw him every day in the week. It was also reported that she and Ferenczi had kissed during the course of treatment, but how much and how far has not been disclosed. [3]

Ferenczi's willingness to cross traditional psychotherapeutic boundaries established by Freud was largely what led Freud ultimately to disown Ferenczi as his heir apparent. Of course, Freud was no prude. On this matter, he was more concerned about bad press than faulty practice. Unquestionably, had Ferenczi's fluid physical boundaries with patients become a psychoanalytic tradition, psychoanalysis in the libidinally-phobic U.S. would have been smothered in its crib.

For the remaining decade of his life, Freud never assigned himself another heir. Ernest Jones would have been the most likely candidate, it would seem, but Freud never quite warmed up to him, and did not trust him. Jones, however—along with the former American ambassador to France, William C. Bullitt, Jr.—did do much to negotiate with German authorities Freud's removal from Nazi Austria to France and then to England, thereby saving his life barely a year prior to the war. After Freud was delivered to England in 1938, Freud's three sisters ultimately died in German concentration camps. Two were executed in a gas chamber. One died of an illness. Freud himself died in 1939, simultaneously with the start of the war, bereft of an assigned heir, which was in retrospect just as well.

Returning home from Budapest in the autumn of 1928, Thompson, as promised, shared with Sullivan what she had learned from Ferenczi, seemingly playing a role as a stand-in training analyst to Sullivan as he had requested. She used whatever she had learned from Ferenczi that was useful to her. Relating to Sullivan what she had experienced and learned from Ferenczi was to be expected. But to attempt to duplicate her analytic experience with Sullivan himself was likely a bridge too far, although there is little data to go on; the project of introducing to Sullivan the Ferenczi psychoanalytic approach through practice was seemingly truncated, or possibly even aborted, as might have been predicted. When Thompson castigated Sullivan for his profligate spending, her judgment negatively affected their project of teaching and learning about Ferenczi's psychoanalytic approach, and discord resulted. His counter was that his dear friend was "too bourgeois" in her values, lifestyle, and spending practices. The rift over Sullivan's financial extravagances had the earmarks of a marital couple fighting, but the conflict did not seem to hobble their strong friendship in the long run. In the end, Thompson was proved correct; Sullivan was forced to declare bankruptcy in 1931. Even so, Thompson helped bail Sullivan out of his financial problems by loaning him large sums of money; loans for which there is no evidence of repayment. Knowing Sullivan, he was likely never financially flush enough to pay her back.

Yet Clara Thomson remained close to Sullivan for the rest of his life. She was a central figure in both the Miracle Club in Baltimore, and its later replica, the Zodiac Club in New York City, which consisted of some of Sullivan's and Thompson's closest social, professional, and intellectual friends. Their social lives were populated by Billy Silverberg, Eric Fromm, Karen Horney, David Rioch, Sullivan's adopted son Jimmie on occasion, and others.

After filing for bankruptcy, as Thompson had predicted, Sullivan then went on a wide personal appeal to friends for money to cover his $27,000 debt. Thompson loaned him $3,050; Brill loaned him $500. Ross McClure Chapman, his dear friend and former administrator at Sheppard Pratt, loaned him $500; and a certain Dr. David M. Levy of Croton-on-Hudson loaned him $7,000. There were likely others. It's doubtful that Sullivan ever paid back any of it; Sullivan had no respect for money, his or anyone else's. Data shows that Sullivan's $27,000 in debts in 1932 was equivalent to about $450,000 in 2021 dollars. (A U.S. dollar in 1932 held the value of about $17 in 2021. That meant that Thompson herself loaned Sullivan the 2021 equivalent of about $52,000.) [4]

Money was not the only source of Sullivan's trouble. On October 29, 1931, Sullivan wrote quite a revealing letter to William Alanson White's wife, Lola, for whom he had a great deal of admiration and regard, which seemed to be reciprocal. He confided in her the dismalness of his affairs since he had resigned from Sheppard. From the tone of the letter, one can see that Sullivan believed that she actually liked him even if White himself was at best ambivalent toward him. He wrote, "I hear that you were inquiring of my address.... It's a very genuine pleasure to receive this assurance of some surviving interest in my for some considerable time extraordinarily inconsequential existence.... I have committed myself to the writing of a book, for which I have no trace of the incredible talent of Dr. White...." [5]

It is difficult to know what to make of this letter, full of self-abnegation, and of appreciation, especially of White's wife. The letter writer was the same man who had revolutionized psychotherapy through his work with schizophrenics in his eight years at Sheppard Pratt. It seems clear, however, that Sullivan was struggling both with money problems and with the direction of his life. It was a few more years—around 1937, the year White died—until Sullivan got new clarity for a direction that would make his last decade quite productive. It may have been no coincidence that Sullivan found his sea legs only after White's death. The relationship had all the marks of a troubled father-son relationship.

❖ ❖ ❖

Those who belonged to Sullivan's circle later acquired the epithet, *Neo-Freudian*. The origins of this label do not seem to be known, but it is a rather misleading sobriquet. The Neo-Freudians were simply Freudians who took off on their own path. In my view, there are only two credible classifications of psychiatry related to Freud—"Freudian" and "anti-Freudian"—and Sullivan was a Freudian. What does the prefix "neo" add? Of course, he did not follow Freud slavishly; what person of integrity and self-regard would be so unoriginal? He modified Freudian theory and practice, as anyone of any substance certainly did and does. No competent therapist in his or her right mind mimicked Freud or attempted to became a carbon copy of him. In fact, Freud did not even mimic himself. He was continually modifying both his theory and practice. Those who followed him had every warrant to modify their own theory and practice, and to do so repeatedly, as did Sullivan and his cohorts.

The most significant changes to Freud's therapeutic approach were Sullivan's de-emphasis on libido theory, and shift toward a psychology of interpersonal relationships, with a laser focus on the interpersonal dimension. This was no cosmic shift away from Freud, but merely a fine-tuning and a complementary manifestation of Freud's own approach. What inspired Sullivan to make this shift was the fact that he worked mostly with psychotics, whereas Freud avoided psychotics; he thought they were untreatable psychoanalytically, therefore attended only to neurotics, or so-called "normal people." Sullivan thought that the couch and the free association method were not fruitful for schizophrenics. Even some simple neurotics find the couch intimidating, as in "what am I supposed to be talking to myself about today?" Sullivan disposed of the couch, and replaced it with two chairs positioned at right angles so that the default position would not be an in-your-face, face-to-face stare. He did from time to time turn his head to look patients in the face, or in the eye, but he believed that anything close to a stare at a schizophrenic patient was counterproductive. Sullivan's revised office architecture was likely more productive than the couch, even for normal neurotics, and certainly so for borderlines…and even for trainees in psychotherapy.

❖ ❖ ❖

In New York City, Thompson attended an art exhibit of the works of a Budapest painter, Henry Major. There is no evidence confirming that Thompson and Major had met earlier during her long stays in Budapest, during which time she took an American lover. For sure, the new romance was a fast-moving affair. Major was said to be married and was restrained from divorcing. Very soon, he moved in with Thompson and remained with her for the remainder of his life. It was said to have been a very happy decade-long relationship. Major died in late 1948. Biographer Maurice Green wrote that Thompson never fully surmounted her grief at the loss of Major. It is noteworthy that Thompson lost arguably the two most important men in life within months of each other, Sullivan and Major. [6]

❖ ❖ ❖

The common ground of both Sullivan and Ferenczi was their attention to the interpersonal dimension, rather than Freud's primary attention to the individual unconscious. This distinction was not as oppositional as many have claimed. Both the unconscious and the interpersonal are always in play, except perhaps for patients housed in the back wards of psychiatric hospitals. The question is a matter of emphasis and focus.

Transference is distortion in a relationship. Sullivan felt the need to invent a new word for it, *parataxic distortion*. In terms of etymology, Sullivan's replacement is arguably more accurate. However, "parataxic" never caught on, and transference continues in common usage. Transference was not invented by psychoanalysis, but merely identified by it. Transference is defined precisely as consisting of the irrational attitudes and feelings that accrue in a relationship, attitudes toward and thoughts about the other based not on clear observation and perception, but on data rooted in the imagination of the one imagining. Simply liking someone does not constitute transference as such; the attraction must have an irrational dimension. Transference implies distortion, such as liking or hating someone irrationally because that person is reminiscent of, say, one's mother. One can learn to modify one's transferential tendencies through therapy, analysis, or even through serious self-reflection. The latter of the three is how Freud himself learned.

For Ferenczi, sexual attraction between therapist and patient must not be covered up or ignored. To do so would imply guilt, shame, or denial. Nor did Ferenczi believe that all sexual attraction between therapist and patient was transference; attraction can be healthy, free of a neurotic character. He argued that such attractions should not be hidden, because they would be obvious in any case. Truth telling is essential in a therapeutic relationship.

Freud himself was no sexual puritan. His wife's sister, Minna Bernays, who lived with the family in a bedroom that adjoined the master bedroom, was Freud's likely sexual partner for decades. The details of their relationship were obvious to some, including Jung, but only became established as fact in the twenty-first century. For more than a century, Freud's sexual relationship with his sister-in-law was denied in psychoanalytic circles, on the order of another "emperor's new clothes" syndrome. This disregard of facts revealed an astonishing naïveté on the part of all of Freud's followers and biographers who cast him in the psychoanalytic myth as a bourgeois middle class monogamist. Furthermore, as an antiquarian Freud would have been quite aware of Biblical, Mishnaic and Talmudic tolerance of polygamy, or more precisely polygyny. Being a non-practicing Jew, Freud would have felt no need to commit to modern Western (since the eleventh century)

Ashkenazic Jewish practice of monogamy, which diverged from Biblical and Talmudic legislation and its permission for polygyny. Sephardic Jews in the East continue to tolerate polygamy. Recently, Peter Gay admirably disclosed his change of view about Freud's relationship with Minna in light of the new data. What tipped the scales of opinion was the discovery by a reporter of the registration book of a resort hotel in question, where Freud registered Minna and himself as "Sigmund Freud and spouse." The inclination by so many scholars to believe that Freud's many long summer vacations through the decades alone with Minna were platonic in nature revealed a certain naïveté which has now been exposed for what it was. [7]

Presumably Minna provided a sexual outlet for Freud that he could not have found in a regular affair, given the danger of being exposed by anti-Semitic Austrians as a Jewish sexual pervert, a common theme in the anti-Semitic German and Austrian culture.

❖ ❖ ❖

In the view of both Freud and Ferenczi, the analyst must love the patient. Psychoanalysis was after all, according to Freud, "the cure though love"—not necessarily love expressed physically or genitally, but love nevertheless. For Ferenczi, genital contact was seemingly no more than a public relations problem. For Freud, such love must be controlled by abstinence and must not be physically consummated. If so, it would become potentially a catastrophic public relations problem, but it was more. It was a violation of Freud's theoretical position of sexual abstinence in the psychoanalytic relationship. He contended that the psychoanalyst must not benefit emotionally from the treatment, a contention from which Ferenczi dissented. How far Ferenczi went in "loving patients" is not entirely clear, but it is clear that he kissed patients, and was freewheeling in other physical ways, such as switching roles with patients. His libertinism deeply disturbed Freud, leading to a separation and ultimately a complete rejection of Ferenczi by Freud. Clara Thompson did not seem to be concerned about any of that. As for Thompson's relationship with Ferenczi, we do not know details beyond the report of their kissing.

❖ ❖ ❖

Freud held the view that psychoanalysis was ineffective with psychotics, and he was certainly correct regarding the style of psychoanalysis that Freud employed. Patient and therapist might sit for an hour, with no words spoken. The distant therapist, with the patient on the couch, is not a likely a treatment model accessible to psychotics, as Freud himself found out. But neither Sullivan nor Ferenczi would allow a 50-minute silence. They would very quickly attempt to get something going relationally, one way or another.

Ferenczi contended that analysis becomes an actively protecting mother, and that the patient must experience childhood love—from the therapist if necessary—before the patient can realize what he missed. Thus, the analyst becomes not only an indulgent but actively protecting authority but also a parental substitute. When I myself entered into psychoanalytically oriented clinical pastoral supervision under Armen Jorjorian in 1967, I experienced Jorjorian both as a correcting father and an indulgent mother, and we developed a deep—and for me—therapeutic bond. When patients or trainees distrust their therapists or experience undue aggression from them, the therapy ceases.

❖ ❖ ❖

Sullivan contended that identification with the enemy was a way to master the environment. An identification with the aggressor was a way to create an ego defense. Think of Germans, and others under Hitler—even some

Jews—who joined forces with the hostile power. The enemy feared from the outside has reappeared inside the self.

Regarding countertransference, Sullivan opined that when the therapist is annoyed, it is difficult to assess whether the patient is unconsciously provoking, or whether the source of annoyance is in the therapist's own personal life. If there are disturbances in the therapist's own life, it is important for the therapist to be aware of them and to frankly acknowledge them to the patient.

On the question of whether it is possible for a therapist to fall in love—non-neurotically—with a patient, and to then maintain a healthy relationship with that patient, the answer must be yes. The principal caveat is that the pattern already set is that one person is the therapist/consultant/analyst providing a service, and the other person is a recipient, indebted to the consultant for what is received. Such a pattern is the essential nature of a therapeutic relationship. When the therapist becomes related to the patient on an intimate personal basis, the parameters and assumptions about the relationship are significantly undermined, and the relationship will find itself on thin ice. No marriage or friendship in which one is the wise authority and the other is the recipient of that wisdom will prosper as a peer relationship. It is difficult to undo the terms of a beginning. The imbalance must be reconstructed for any authentic peer relationship to prosper. It can be a daunting task to remodel a human relationship and radically alter the assumptions with which the relationship began. The second reason why a sexual relationship with a patient is ill advised, is that sexual relations outside of monogamy in any culture immersed in Christianity will always carry the taint of the unethical. Thus, if a therapist is determined to pursue a personal or love relationship with a patient or student, she or he should refer the patient elsewhere for the pursuit of therapy or analysis.

One of the problems Freud had with Ferenczi was that the latter diluted the professional boundary and distance between patient and therapist, sometimes even changing seats and reversing roles so that the patient played the role of therapist. And, of course, Ferenczi's openness to physical contact between patient and therapist went against the grain of Freudian psychoanalysis. Ferenczi, of course, deserves credit for his courage, even audacity, in striking out on his own in this respect, breaking glass. But one can also understand Freud's concern about Ferenczi's lack of so-called professionalism, and about how this would be received by the public. Such fluidity of roles opens the door to a sexually physical relationship between patient and therapist, something that Ferenczi seemed to feel free to engage in, and to which Freud was adamantly in opposition, leading to the rupture of their relationship. Freud's position was founded on the presumption that clinical work requires a certain distance. On the other hand, such boundaries do not seem to be fixed in stone. Interpersonal intimacy resides on a spectrum.

The prohibition of sexual relations with patients is not premised on the proposition that sex is evil. It is based on the premise that one should get what one pays for. If a therapist is gratifying him or herself, then he or she should not ask for a fee, or maybe the patient should be paid for services rendered. Or in Sullivan's own words, which he reports to have said after being propositioned by a patient, "I know I would enjoy it, but it would gum up the works terribly and the work is more important, we have more important things to do." When a patient persisted, he would say something like, "Sure, I think zonal pleasures are alright but I am selling an expert service, not having a good time." [8]

❖ ❖ ❖

Clara Thompson biographer Maurice R. Green wrote that she shifted the focus of psychoanalysis from Freud's libido theory toward ego psychology and an interpersonal focus, which was not a cosmic change, but a shift of focus. Clearly she was following Sullivan. [10]

When a powerful positive transference develops in the first hour, one can look for trouble ahead, according to Sullivan. Mostly, when an aggressive, manipulative woman finds a passive, masochistic male analyst, one who "really understands her," the therapeutic relationship will be subverted, says Sullivan. He added, a perfectly analyzed therapist is likely nowhere to be found; a healthy humility is probably the best safeguard against grandiosity.

❖ ❖ ❖

Freud sought to make the personality of the therapist as indistinct and inconspicuous as possible in the eyes of the patient. That was a large part of the substance of the extended training analysis. Sullivan took a different stance on this; he was very much a "person" in the analytic process, reacting to the patient in a variety of ways, with humor, sarcasm, physicality, and so forth. But each man was, to some extent, flexible in his overall posture. Freud is reported to have given money to destitute patients and to have invited certain patients to dinner with his family after a session. He also sought, by his own account, surreptitiously to encounter a former patient, Elizabeth von R, at a social gathering in order to discover if she were well subsequent to his treatment. Freud seems to have been quite flexible in practice, if not in theory, as to his manner of relating to patients. Clara Thompson and Sándor Ferenczi each assumed even more flexible roles; especially Ferenczi, who was spontaneous and at times wildly innovative, to the dismay of and ultimately the rejection of Freud. Sometimes he would pursue patients across town when he heard someone was in trouble. Ferenczi on occasion would even confess to patients the mistakes he had made in the therapy process.

Thompson wrote that from 1930 on, she, Fromm-Reichmann, and Sullivan also made a point of sharing with patients their mistakes. No longer would they take the position in relation to a patient, "You are angry with me because you are actually angry at your father/mother/etc." Thompson added that all therapists needed to do this. When things are not going well with our automobiles or radios, we have them checked. So should we self-check as therapists, she argued. If things are not going well with a patient, we must not automatically assume that the source of the difficulty is in the patient.

The Sullivan position, followed by Thompson, was that a persistent attitude of good will and genuine concern for the patient's welfare will eventually penetrate a patient's mistrust and despair. But it must be genuine. The therapist must really like his fellow human being to be helpful to him.

In the nexus with patients, the therapist must be able to accept hostility without feeling that security is threatened. One does not have to enjoy being attacked, as would a sadomasochist, but must tolerate it and attempt to understand it. The deepest motive is the search for intimacy, according to Thompson.

It is noteworthy that, as far as the written record goes, Thompson had no awareness of the clinical pastoral movement under Anton Boisen. Since she was very close to Sullivan, that is curious, if true. Boisen was publishing numerous papers and monographs in the psychiatric arena. Perhaps Boisen was not a point of interest to her in her world, particularly since she had rebelled against the Christian religiosity in her family of origin, and abandoned her initial dream of becoming a Baptist missionary to China. Freud saw the beginnings of the women's movement and called it "penis envy." Perhaps he did not realize that penis envy was a necessary step toward a new orientation.

All transition states are anxiety-producing until a new solution is found. Of course, men also have been negatively affected by this restlessness and newfound assertiveness in women. However, Freud supported, trained, and endorsed a number of women psychoanalysts, his daughter Anna among them.

The analysis of many attractive women has come to grief on just this situation, where the therapist—possibly guilty because of his own thoughts—did not dare deal with the direct situation, but insisted on talking only of transference, although not his own. At the same time, under his professional mask, he continued to enjoy the sight and presence of the female patient. Furthermore, therapists generally agree that even falling in love in everyday life usually has some transference element.

The story is told that David Rioch, one of Sullivan's friends and colleague, and husband of Margaret Rioch, attempted to tease Sullivan openly at a faculty social gathering at Chestnut Lodge in 1943. After a few drinks, Rioch said to Sullivan, "Harry, why the blazes can't you write so people can understand you?" Sullivan is reported to have exploded, left the party and did not return. [9] Undoubtedly, he was sensitive about his writing ability and perhaps knew it was too late in life to improve in that skill. But a skill in writing is not the alpha and omega of a competent psychotherapist, or even a competent thinker. Perhaps Sullivan's own awareness of his lack of talent in that arena is the reason he published only one book in his lifetime, though the more likely reason was that he feared full public disclosure of his idiosyncratic work with patients. Anyone who wishes to fathom Sullivan by an easier route than reading Sullivan directly can come close to Sullivan by way of Clara Thompson, Dorothy Blitsten, and Frieda Fromm-Reichmann, each of whom was devoted to Sullivan and subscribed to his theories and practice.

1. Perry, Helen Swick. (1982). *Psychiatrist of America: The Life of Harry Stack Sullivan.* Cambridge, MA: The Belknap Press of Harvard University, pp. 201–2.

2. Sorge, Giovanni. (Fall 2012). "Jung's Presidency of the International General Medical Society of Psychotherapy: New Insights." *Jung Journal: Culture & Psyche*, Vol. 6, No. 4, pp. 31–53; and "Jung Played a Role in

Early Third Reich" Letter to the Editor by Nathaniel S. Lehrman. (May 3, 1988). *The New York Times*, section A, p. 34.

3. Green, Maurice R., ed. (1964). *Interpersonal Psychoanalysis: The Selected Papers of Clara M. Thompson*. New York: Basic Books, Inc. Publishers, p. 336; see also Robert S. Wallerstein, (1995). *The Talking Cures*. Yale University Press, New Haven, p. 21.

4. Perry, *op. cit.*, p. 322.

5. Ibid., p. 323.

6. Green, *op. cit.*, p. 371.

7. New York Times, December 24, 2006. For more historical context see *The Poisoning of Eros: Sexual Values in Conflict,* Raymond J. Lawrence, Augustine Moore Press, 1989, pp. 18–25.

8. Kvarnes, *op. cit.*, p. 216.

9. Vande Kemp, Hendrika. (2004). *Harry Stack Sullivan (1892–1949): Hero, Ghost, and Muse*. In *The Psychotherapy Patient*, Vol 13. Philadelphia: The Haworth Press, Inc., p. 24.

CHAPTER 11

The Last Word

಄∞ಀ

Harry Stack Sullivan and Anton T. Boisen were very much alike on matters of importance. They each came out of nowhere, unsponsored, with little backing and bereft of money. Each was socially unpredictable, but extremely kindly and compassionate in certain contexts. Each was quite idiosyncratic. They each survived involuntary institutional psychiatric treatment. Each was happy that he was spared a frontal lobotomy or other invasive psychiatric interventions.

Ultimately, both men found their way into psychotherapeutic work, Sullivan via medicine, and Boisen via religion. Neither man was typical of his profession. And both men radically altered the thinking and the direction of their respective disciplines, psychiatry and religious ministry. Each viewed their respective disciplines as very much overlapping. They each viewed their vocations as that of *the cure of souls.*

They each doggedly addressed with compassion the suffering of their own generation, more particularly the suffering of those who experienced, as they themselves did, episodic schizophrenia. They each practiced and taught the skills of healing of similarly broken persons, and they were each motivated to do this through their identification with persons who experienced a similar condition. Most peculiarly, though they did escape the harshest treatments of early 20th-century psychiatry, neither Sullivan nor Boisen seemed to find fullness of healing for themselves. It can be said about both men that they did for others what they could not fully do for themselves.

Both Sullivan and Boisen radically revolutionized their chosen professions. American psychiatry was never the same after Sullivan. It was deepened and broadened. And the work of religious professionals was never the same after Boisen. They each became healers rather than simply ideologues or technicians. Both men had a history of being devalued by the leadership of their particular professions.

In the world of psychiatry and psychoanalysis, the name of Harry Stack Sullivan virtually disappeared from the radar the moment he died in January, 1949. The American Psychoanalytic Association aggressively and immediately divested itself of any association with Sullivan, the psychiatrist, and his radical ideas. [1] But the few notables who knew him personally—specifically Helen Swick Perry, Clara Thompson, David McKenzie Rioch, Margaret Rioch, Patrick Mullahy, Janet MacKenzie Rioch, Dexter M. Bullard, Mabel Blake Cohen, Dorothy Blitsten, Robert G. Kvarnes, Otto Will and Lester Havens—energetically worked to preserve the memory and legacy of the authentic Harry Stack Sullivan. And in the twenty-first century, F. Barton Evans and the Italian psychoanalyst Marco Conci have, in their published works, continued the mission of preserving the genius of Sullivan for posterity. Boisen had strong allies in the Council for Clinical Training that he founded, but as he aged he lost connection with many of them, in part because of his apparent mental decline.

Sullivan has been appreciated more by the Europeans, most notably the Italians, than by his own countryman. The original "Florence Neo-Freudian Institute" in Italy was subsequently renamed the "Sullivan Institute." [2] There seems to be no public memorial for Sullivan in the U.S. aside from the rather unheralded and isolated "Chenango County Harry Stack Sullivan Mental Health Clinic," which was named in his honor 28 years after his death. On the other hand, Boisen's name continued to be held in esteem posthumously, but the matters he fought for were ultimately detached from his name by the organization he founded.

However, contemporary psychiatry is profoundly shaped for the better by Sullivan, even though his name is missing. Boisen's fate has been quite different. By the latter decades of the twentieth century about all the typical pastoral clinician knew about Boisen was how to spell his name. He is remembered, as if he were a beneficent grandfather, but his profound contribution to the potential healing dimension of pastoral work is for the most part lost. And it may never be recovered by the mainstream.

Sullivan was despised by a large swath of his peers, from whom many garnered so much. Boisen was simply forgotten as if he were irrelevant. But Sullivan did leave a permanent mark on psychiatry. Boisen's contribution to pastoral work has up to now been mostly forgotten or erased. By the onset of the twenty-first century most of the alleged followers of Boisen had morphed into peddlers of spirituality, prayer, and religion, the very antithesis of Boisen's life work. [3]

In a letter to Carl Jung in 1906, Freud wrote that psychoanalysis was essentially "a cure through love". [4] Boisen and Sullivan clearly followed that directive in their respective patient work, and did so even more explicitly than Freud himself. Sullivan, and Boisen with him, shifted much of his attention away from the unconscious to give attention to the social self and the interpersonal. The quarter-century working partnership between Sullivan and Boisen might have been a harbinger of a future cooperative spirit between all humanistic psychiatry and all humanistic religion. But the fulfillment of that vision will have to wait for a brighter day.

---

1. Perry, Helen Swick. (1982). *Psychiatrist of America: The Life of Harry Stack Sullivan*. Cambridge, MA: The Belknap Press of Harvard University, p. 327.

2. Conci, Marco. (2019). *Freud, Sullivan, Mitchell, Bion, and the Multiple Voices of International Psychoanalysis*. New York: IPBooks, p. 170.

3. For an analysis of the current state of the discipline, see in particular, Fitchett, George and Steve Nolan, eds. (2015). *Spiritual Care and Practice, Case Studies in Healthcare Chaplaincy* and also Fitchett and Nolan's *Case Studies in Spiritual Care*, 2018; and my rebuttals: *Nine Clinical Cases: The Soul of Pastoral Care and Counseling* (2015) and *Nine More Clinical Cases: Case Studies in Clinical Pastoral Care, Counseling, and Psychotherapy* (2020). New York: CPSP Press.

4. Freud in a letter to Jung, 1906.

www.ingramcontent.com/pod-product-compliance
Lightning Source LLC
Chambersburg PA
CBHW062130020426
42335CB00013B/1163